Francesco Satolli

Loyalty to Church and State

the mind of His Excellency Francis archbishop Satolli

Francesco Satolli

Loyalty to Church and State
the mind of His Excellency Francis archbishop Satolli

ISBN/EAN: 9783337260415

Printed in Europe, USA, Canada, Australia, Japan

Cover: Foto ©Lupo / pixelio.de

More available books at **www.hansebooks.com**

LOYALTY TO

CHURCH AND STATE.

THE MIND OF

His Excellency, Francis Archbishop Satolli,

APOSTOLIC DELEGATE.

"Justice, charity, and loyalty to Church and Country
are always and everywhere, true characteristics of Papal
diplomacy."—*Carroll Institute Address,* p. 100.

BALTIMORE :

JOHN MURPHY & COMPANY,

1895.

AUTHORIZED EDITION.

EDITED BY THE VERY REV. J. R. SLATTERY,

ST. JOSEPH'S SEMINARY,

BALTIMORE, MD.

☞ Proceeds toward the support of St. Joseph's
Seminary and Epiphany Apostolic College for training
missionaries to the colored people.

"All intelligent men are agreed, and we ourselves have with pleasure intimated, that America seems destined for greater things. Now, it is our wish that the Catholic Church should not only share in, but help to bring about, this prospective greatness. We deem it right and proper that she should, by availing herself of the opportunities daily presented to her, keep equal step with the Republic in the march of improvement, at the same time striving to the utmost, by her virtue and her institutions, to aid in the rapid growth of the States. Now, she will attain both these objects the more easily and abundantly, in proportion to the degree in which the future shall find her constitution perfected. But what is the meaning of the Apostolic Delegation, or what is its ultimate aim except to bring about that the constitution of the Church shall be strengthened, her discipline better fortified."

Encyclical of Leo XIII to the Archbishops
and Bishops in the United States.

TABLE OF CONTENTS.

7

PART X.—ON THE TRAINING OF YOUTH.

PART XI.—LETTERS.

PREFACE

BY

HIS EMINENCE, JAMES CARDINAL GIBBONS.

———

The speeches and addresses contained in this volume were delivered by His Excellency, the Most Rev. Francis Satolli, Archbishop of Lepanto, Delegate Apostolic to the United States, since his arrival in America, and are published with his sanction. Archbishop Satolli's first appearance among us was in the fall of 1889, when he came as the representative of Leo XIII, to the twin ceremonies that marked the end of the first century of the American Church; the centenary of the American Hierarchy and the inauguration of the Catholic University. The discourse he pronounced at the University is not recorded in this volume, but is impressed in the memory of those who were privileged at the time to listen to the finished periods of Ciceronian Latin in which it was spoken.

11

In 1892 he returned to our shores as Papal Commissioner to the World's Fair, and in this capacity was honored by the Federal Government and the World's Fair Directory, with the marks of distinction and courtliness due to the office he filled and the august dignitary he represented. A few months afterward, in January, 1893, the Apostolic Delegation was established by His Holiness, and the Papal Commissioner became the Apostolic Delegate.

Then came to him from bishops and priests in various parts of the country, invitations to ecclesiastical ceremonies; receptions and banquets were given him; it was mostly on those occasions that the following addresses were delivered. Unfortunately, the speeches he made west of St. Paul, at Helena, Butte, Tacoma, Portland, San Francisco, Salt Lake City were not preserved; though some of them, notably those given at Tacoma, San Francisco, Salt Lake City and Butte, were judged by the clergymen who accompanied His Excellency on that trip, to be equal to the best delivered by him in the cities of the Atlantic coast.

We can well imagine how the revelations of

that long voyage, the vast extent of the country, the glories of the plains and mountains, the natural resources of the Western land, the rapidity of its colonization, the progress of its young churches, the magical rise of its new cities, the magnificent scenery of the Pacific Coast, the warm-hearted welcome of its inhabitants Catholic and non-Catholic, must have been an inspiration to one born and bred amid the staid and ancient civilization of Italy with its past centuries of historic ancestry. The travels of the Delegate, had the advantage of bringing him in contact not only with the physical, but, also with the ecclesiastical and mental characteristics of our vast country. Thus, he learned to know the field in which he was called to work, and the people learned to know his features, and his thoughts, fears, hopes of our present and our future.

All this is reflected in the following pages; for, though the English dress of these addresses is not of the Delegate's make, the ideas are all his. His usual method was to dictate in Italian or Latin; his Secretary or one of his retinue translated into English and submitted the translation for his approval. On some occasions, he has read the English speech himself, oftener it was read for him in his presence to the audience. These explanations account for the unequalness and difference of style on the one hand, for the consistency and unity of thought on the other.

Looking at the matter of these addresses, a wide field is covered. The Papacy, the constitution of the Church, the spirit of American institutions and their harmony with the spirit of Catholicity, the unification through the Church of the various national elements that go to make up the American people, education, schools, public and private, religious associations and confraternities, interests local to the place where, for the time being, he speaks, such mainly are the topics dealt with by the Most Reverend Orator.

The broad spirit in which they are treated, is the most prominent feature of those addresses. The world knows what manner of man is Leo XIII. how wide his grasp, how keen his insight, how lofty his conception of civil government, how warm his interest in the essay, so far successful, we are making of Democracy, how conciliatory his attitude towards all that is just, noble, fair and morally good everywhere and

anywhere among non-Catholics throughout the
world. This breadth of mind and sympathy of
heart as wide as human nature itself, are the
result of training in the Philosophy and Theology
that have their highest and most finished expression in the Angel of the Schools, St. Thomas
of Aquin.

As the foremost student in the world to-day of
that great master, as the favorite pupil since
earliest years of that great Pope, Francis Satolli
could not be narrow of mind and cold of heart in
this land where the civil and religious future of
the world is being wrought out, if the most far-
seeing minds, not only of America, but of Europe
are to be believed; in the presence of this people
into the racial formation of which enter contri-
butions from all the world, into the civil formation of which the philosophy and experience of
centuries combine to rear a political edifice
such as the past has not seen, the Republic
of the United States. Nor has he been narrow
or cold, as the reader may judge for himself.
Quite the contrary. It is those addresses not
less than his fairness and justice in the administration of his office that have endeared him to

the hearts of the American public, irrespective of religious belief.

This volume is edited by the Very Rev. J. R. Slattery, well known throughout the United States for his zeal in the cause of the Negro Missions. It was to show his sympathy with this noble, but too much neglected cause that the Delegate Apostolic chose Father Slattery for the task of editing his addresses. The profit of the sale of this volume will go to the work to which this noble-hearted priest has devoted his life. We trust that this consideration will appeal to the American reading public, and that the missionary end in view no less than the intrinsic merits of the book will assure its financial success.

J. CARD. GIBBONS.

MILE-STONES IN A LIFETIME.

FRANCIS SATOLLI,

Archbishop of Lepanto, and Delegate Apostolic to the United States.

1839. Born July 21, 1839, at Marsciano, a small town in the Diocese of Perugia, Italy. His ancestors are known up to the 15th century as his family tree shows; they belonged to the "Patriciate" of Perugia. He attended the primary schools in the same town of Marsciano, and in

1853. Sent to the Seminary of Perugia, where he studied literature, having as a teacher, his brother John-Baptist, an excellent scholar and famous preacher.

In the same seminary, he was taught philosophy and its different branches, having as professor of philosophy the Rev. Dr. Pecci, a brother of the present Pope Leo XIII.

In the third year of his philosophical course, he sustained a public thesis in analytical geometry.

2

During the course of theology he received all the sacred orders from the Archbishop of Perugia, the present Pope, including the sacred order of the priesthood.

1862. Ordained Priest in 1862.

1862 Taught letters for one year, and philosophy for the
to   remaining years in the same seminary ; he was
1870.   also at this time rector of a parish in the city of
         Perugia.

1870 Taught in the Benedictine Abbey of Monte Cassino
to   with his Ordinary's permission, meanwhile exer-
1875.   cising the ministry of preaching in his Diocese.

1875 Rector of one of the most important parishes of that
to   Diocese in Marsciano.

1880.   He was a member, and afterwards the director
         of the " Academy of St. Thomas" founded in
         Perugia by Card. Pecci. It was a rule to hold
         monthly meetings in this academy, at which its
         members were accustomed to give lectures and
         discuss philosophical subjects. Their aim was to
         cultivate St. Thomas' doctrines, and to adapt them
         to the methods and trend of modern philosophy.

            During the same time he published some pam-
         phlets on different philosophical subjects. He
         continued to exercise the ministry of preaching
         in obedience to the wish of the Archbishop of
         Perugia.

1880. Called to Rome by the Holy Father to teach Theology in the Propaganda College. He filled this chair until 1892, adopting for his text-book the "Summa theologica" of Saint Thomas. The happy results derived from this method are well known everywhere. In order to make the study of St. Thomas easier for his pupils, he composed a work in five volumes. Their subject matter are various points of doctrine, luminously explained in accordance with St. Thomas' teachings.

1884. Appointed rector of the Greek College in Rome. He filled this office until 1886. During his administration he attended to the moral improvement of said college by awakening and fostering among the students the true ecclesiastic spirit.

By building another wing, connected with the old edifice, through generous pecuniary gifts received from the Holy Father, he enlarged the college facilities.

Finally, he obtained permission from the Holy Father to entrust the administration of this college to a religious community.

1885. Made a Canon of St. John Lateran and Domestic Prelate to His Holiness.

1886. Appointed President of the Academy of the Noble ecclesiastics (Academia dei Nobili ecclesiastici).

In this Academy he taught *"Jus publicum
ecclesiasticum,"* and published two small works
on the same subject.

1888. Consecrated Archbishop, and made titular of Lepanto.

During all the time spent in Rome he was an
active member of the " Theological Academy of
St. Thomas," regularly attending its sessions and
enriching its archives with the productions of his
pen.   While in Rome, he continued to exercise
the ministry of preaching, speaking in the principal churches, always with success.

1889. Sent to the United States of America by the Holy
Father as His Representative at the Centennial
Celebration of the American Hierarchy and at
the inauguration of the Catholic University.

1892. Sent a second time by the Holy Father to America.
What has happened since then is well known.

————————

LETTER.

WASHINGTON, D. C., *Nov.* 13, 1894.

V. REV. J. R. SLATTERY,
  Rector of St. Joseph's Seminary
    for the Colored Missions.

Very Rev. and Dear Father: — There is no doubt that eagerness to rush into print is one of the characteristic features of this age; hence the vast multitude of books, pamphlets and papers given to the public without any regard to a high aim or a noble purpose. For, some seek merely prominence and public fame, while others have for their purpose the intellectual and moral betterment of their fellow-men, seeking to lead them to the true, the good, and the beautiful; the noblest objects of our faculties.

" Nature is an open-book for discoverers, while written books are prepared for scholars," is a

trite saying. But there are only a few men
who are gifted with the genius of original discovery: it follows, therefore, as a logical conclusion that books should be supplied as a means
of instruction for the multitude in proportion to
their progress in civilization.

In former ages books were few in number,
but large, voluminous and destined to live the
life of centuries. To-day. books are innumerable, but many of them diminish both in size
and life.

No one would maintain that it is the size which
gives value to a book. The gospel itself is one of
the smallest books in the world, yet it is worth
more than the famous library of Alexandria.

The kindness and attention with which my
words have universally been received during my
sojourn in America give me reason to hope, that
the publication of this little book, embodying
what I have at different times expressed upon
subjects connected with the interests of our Holy
Church and on education in this country, will not
be unacceptable to public opinion.

It is a source of great consolation to me that
I am enabled by the publication of this little

volume to help on, at least indirectly, the interests of the admirable work to which you have so unselfishly dedicated your life. I have always felt a sympathy and an unconcealed regard for the interests of the colored race in the United States, and I rejoice that I have the opportunity of expressing in this form the interest I take in their welfare.

My dear Father, let us pray that everyone may know how he ought to behave himself in the house of God, which is the Church of the living God, the pillar and ground of truth.

Sincerely Yours in J. C.,

FRANCIS ARCHB. SATOLLI,
Deleg. Apost.

PART I.

On Christian Education.

THE FOURTEEN PROPOSITIONS.

Read and considered in the meeting of the Archbishops at New York, the difficulties answered, and the requisite alterations made, November 17, 1892.

I.

All care must be taken to erect Catholic schools, to enlarge and improve those already established, and to make them equal to the public schools in teaching and in discipline.

Conc. Plen. Balt. III., No. 197, p. 101.

II.

When there is no Catholic school at all, or when the one that is available is little fitted for giving the children an education in keeping with their condition, then the public schools may be attended with a safe conscience, the danger of perversion being rendered remote by opportune remedial and precautionary measures; a matter

27

that is to be left to the conscience and judgment
of the Ordinaries.

Ibid., No. 198, p. 103.

III.

We enact and command that no one shall be
allowed to teach in a parochial school who has
not proven his fitness for the position by previous examination. No priest shall have the right
to employ any teacher, male or female, in his
school, without a certificate of ability or diploma
from the Diocesan Board of Examiners.

Ibid., No. 203, p. 108.

IV.

Normal Schools, as they are called. are to be
established where they are wanting and are evi-
dently necessary.

Ibid., No. 205, p. 110.

V.

We strictly forbid any one, whether Bishop
or Priest, and this is the express prohibition
of the Sovereign Pontiff through the Sacred
Congregation. either by act or by threat to

exclude from the Sacraments as unworthy parents [who choose to send their children to the public schools]. As regards the children themselves, this enactment applies with still greater force.

Ibid., No. 198, p. 104.

Conf. Tit. VI. Cap. I., II.; Tit. VII.

VI.

To the Catholic Church belongs the duty and the divine right of teaching all nations to believe the truth of the Gospel, and to observe whatsoever Christ commanded (*Matth.*, xxviii, 19); in her likewise is vested the divine right of instructing the young in so far as theirs is the Kingdom of Heaven (*Mark*, x, 14) (*Conf. Con. Balt. Pl. III*, No. 194); that is to say, she holds for herself the right of teaching the truths of faith and the law of morals in order to bring up youth in the habits of a Christian life. Hence, absolutely and universally speaking, there is no repugnance in their learning the first elements and the higher branches of the arts and the natural sciences in public schools controlled by the State, whose office it is to provide, maintain and protect everything

by which its citizens are formed to moral goodness, while they live peaceably together, with
a sufficiency of temporal goods, under laws promulgated by civil authority.

For the rest, the provisions of the Council of
Baltimore are yet in force, and, in a general
way, will remain so: to wit: "Not only out of
our paternal love do we exhort Catholic parents,
but we command them, by all the authority we
possess, to procure a truly Christian and Catholic
education for the beloved offspring given them
of God, born again in Baptism unto Christ
and destined for Heaven, to shield and secure
them throughout childhood and youth from the
dangers of a merely worldly education, and
therefore to send them to parochial or other
truly Catholic schools." United with this duty
are the rights of parents, which no civil law or
authority can violate or weaken.

VII.

The Catholic Church in general, and especially the Holy See, far from condemning or
treating with indifference the public schools,
desires rather that, by the joint action of civil

and ecclesiastical authorities, there should be public schools in every State, according as the circumstances of the people require, for the cultivation of the useful arts and natural sciences; but the Catholic Church shrinks from those features of public schools which are opposed to the truth of Christianity and to morality; and since, in the interest of society itself, these objectionable features are removable, therefore, not only the Bishops, but the citizens at large should labor to remove them, in virtue of their own right and in the cause of morality.

VIII.

It is long since the Holy See, after consultation with the Bishops of the United States of America, decreed that parish schools and other institutions under the direction of the Bishops, each according to the conditions of its own diocese, were opportune and necessary for Catholic youth, from the fact that it was held for certain that the public schools bore within themselves a proximate danger to faith and morals, for various reasons (*Conc. Pl. Balt. III.*, No. 194, seq.: App., p. 279); viz: because in the public schools

a purely secular education is given,—inasmuch
as it excludes all teaching of religion,—because
teachers are chosen indiscriminately from every
sect, and no law prevents them from working the
ruin of youth,—so that they are at liberty to instil
errors and the germs of vice in tender minds.
Likewise, certain corruption seemed to impend
from the fact that in these schools, or at least in
many of them, children of both sexes are brought
together for their lessons in the same room.

Wherefore. if it be clear that in a given
locality, owing to the wiser dispositions of public
authorities, or the watchful prudence of School
Board, teachers and parents, the above-named
dangers to faith and morals disappear, then it is
lawful for Catholic parents to send their children
to these schools, to acquire the elements of letters
and arts, provided the parents themselves do not
neglect their most serious duty, and the pastors of
souls put forth every effort, to instruct the children
and train them in all that pertains to Catholic
worship and life.

IX.

It is left to the judgment and the wisdom of
the Ordinaries to decide whether, in a certain

part of their respective dioceses, a parochial school can be built and kept up in a fitting condition, not inferior to the public schools, taking into consideration the temporal condition of the parents, while graver needs for procuring their spiritual welfare and the decent support of the Church are pressing. It will be well, therefore, as was the wont of our forefathers, and as was done in the early days of the Church, to establish weekly classes of Catechism, which all the children of the parish should attend; for the better success of this measure, let the zeal of pastors in fulfilling their duty, and the love of Catholic parents, leave no effort unspared. (Cf. *Conc. Pl. Balt. III.*, No. 198.)

X.

No reproach, either in public or in private, shall be cast upon Catholic parents who send their children to private schools, or to academies where a better education is given under the direction of religious, or of approved and Catholic persons. If they make sufficient provision for the religious training of their children, let them be free to secure in other ways that education which the position of their family requires.

3

XI.

It is greatly to be desired, and will be a most happy arrangement, if the Bishop agree with the civil authorities or with the members of the School Board, to conduct the school with mutual attention and due consideration for their respective rights.

While there are teachers of any description for the secular branches, who are legally inhibited from offending Catholic religion and morality, let the right and duty of the Church obtain of teaching the children Catechism, in order to remove danger to their faith and morals from any quarter whatsoever.

It seems well to quote here the words of our Holy Father Leo XIII. (See the Pope's letter to the Archbishop of New York and to the Bishops of the Province): "We further desire you to strive earnestly that the various local authorities, firmly convinced that nothing is more conducive to the welfare of the common-wealth than religion, should by wise legislation provide that the system of education which is maintained at the public expense, and to which therefore Catholics also contribute their share, be in no way prejudicial to their conscience or religion. For we are persuaded that even your fellow-citizens who differ from us in belief, with their characteristic intelligence and prudence, will readily set aside all suspicions and all views unfavorable to the Catholic Church, and willingly acknowledge her merit, as the one that dispelled the darkness of paganism by the light of the Gospel, and created a new society distinguished by the lustre of christian virtues and by the cultivation of all that refines. We do not think that any one there, after looking into these things clearly, will let Catholic parents be forced to erect and support schools which they cannot use for the instruction of their children."

XII.

As for those Catholic children that in great numbers are educated in the public schools, where now, not without danger, they receive no religious instruction at all, strenuous efforts should be made not to leave them without sufficient and seasonable instruction in Catholic faith and practice. We know by experience that not

all our Catholic children are found in our Catholic
schools. Statistics show that hundreds of thousands of Catholic children in the United States
of America attend schools which are under the
control of State Boards, and in which, for that reason, teachers of every denomination are engaged.
Beyond all doubt, the one thing necessary, i. e.,
religious and moral education according to Catholic principles, is not to be treated either lightly or
with delay, but on the contrary with all earnestness
and energy.

The adoption of one of three plans is recommended, the choice to be made according to
local circumstances in the different States and
various personal relations.

The first consists in an agreement between the
Bishop and the members of the School Board,
whereby they, in a spirit of fairness and good
will, allow the Catholic children to be assembled
during free time and taught the Catechism; it
would also be of the greatest advantage if this
plan were not confined to the primary schools,
but were extended likewise to the high schools
and colleges, in the form of a free lecture.

The second: to have a catechism class outside

the public school building, and also classes of
higher Christian doctrine, where, at fixed times,
the Catholic children would assemble with diligence and pleasure, induced thereto by the authority of their parents, the persuasion of their
pastors, and the hope of praise and rewards.

The third plan does not seem at first sight so
suitable, but is bound up more intimately with
the duty of both parents and pastors. Pastors
should unceasingly urge upon parents that most
important duty, imposed both by natural and
by divine law, of bringing up their children in
sound morality and Catholic faith. Besides,
the instruction of children appertains to the
very essence of the pastoral charge; let the
pastor of souls say to them with the Apostle:
" My little children, of whom I am in labor
again until Christ be formed in you." (*Gal.*,
IV, 19.) Let him have classes of children in the
parish such as have been established in Rome
and many other places, and even in churches in
this country, with very happy results.

Nor let him, with little prudence, show less
love for the children that attend the public
schools than for those that attend the paro-

chial; on the contrary, stronger marks of loving
solitude are to be shown them; the Sunday school
and the hour for Catechism, should be devoted to
them in a special manner. And to cultivate this
field, let the pastor call to his aid other priests,
religious, and even suitable members of the laity,
in order that what is supremely necessary be wanting to no child.

XIII.

For the standing and growth of Catholic
schools, it seems that care should be taken
that the teachers prove themselves qualified,
not only by previous examination before the
Diocesan Board and by a certificate or diploma
received from it, but also by having a teacher's
diploma from the School Board of the State,
awarded after successful examination. This is
urged, first, so as not to appear regardless, without reason, of what public authority requires for
teaching. Secondly, a better opinion of Catholic
schools will be created. Thirdly, greater assurance will be given to parents that in Catholic
schools there is no deficiency to render them
inferior to public schools; that, on the contrary,
everything is done to make Catholic schools equal

to public schools, or even superior. Fourthly, and lastly, we think that this plan would prepare the way for the State to see, along with the recognized and tested fitness of the teachers, that the laws are observed in all matters pertaining to the arts and sciences, to method and pedagogics, and to whatever is ordinarily required to promote the stability and usefulness of the schools.

XIV.

It is necessary that what are called Normal Schools should reach such efficiency in preparing teachers of letters, arts and sciences, that their graduates shall not fail to obtain the Diploma of the State. For the sake of the Catholic cause, let there be among laymen a growing rivalry to take the diploma and doctorate, so that, possessed of the knowledge and qualifications requisite for teaching, they may compete for and honorably obtain, positions in the public Gymnasia, Lyceums and scientific institutions.

The knowledge of truth of every kind, straightforward justice united with charity, the effulgence and appreciation of the liberal arts—these are the bulwarks of the church.

RELIGION AND KNOWLEDGE IN EDUCATION.

In the following masterly address, Mgr. Satolli sets forth the twinship of religion and knowledge in the education of youth.

It was delivered at De La Salle Institute, West 59th St., New York, January 10th, 1895, in the presence of Archbishop Corrigan; Archbishop Ryan, of Philadelphia; Dr. Conroy, Bishop ad Curium; Bishop McFaul, of Trenton; Bishop Burke, of Albany; Bishop Horstmann, of Cleveland; Mgr. Farley, Vicar-General Mooney, Dr. Rooker, Father O'Farrell, Father Kearney, the faculty of the Institute and a very distinguished audience.

At the close of the exercises Father Rooker stepped to the front of the platform and announced that he had been delegated by Mgr. Satolli to read his address for him. He said, translating the Latin of the original :—

Cicero has said that it is the delight of old men to be in the midst of the young, and of young men to cluster around the honored old. Long before Cicero, the inspired author of Ecclesiastes had taught the same truth. By the "old man" of the sacred writer is meant the man who

40

is wise and virtuous, the model and teacher of youth. There are many reasons why the old and young should thus find joy and satisfaction in one another's society. In the first place, the old feel keenly the natural desire to prolong life; they find the greatest pleasure in seeing juvenescent humanity springing up around them, for they seem to behold in the boy the perpetuation of their own existence. Then, too, it gives them great pleasure to communicate to the young what they themselves have learned by hard study and long experience of life.

Their interest and delight, for the most part, arise from the fact that they see founded in the young men about them, the hope of family, society and state. They are inflamed with the desire to see these young men develop such a moral and intellectual temperament as will best assure the future welfare of human kind.

Look at these same reasons from the opposite point of view and you will see in them the motives which incite youth to seek the company of age and to delight in converse with those experienced in virtue and wisdom. Nothing can be more promising, more reassuring than to see a young man draw close to venerable age, that he may learn the lesson of life. These, too, are the reasons why we find so great pleasure in being here to-night and in seeing ourselves surrounded by so many bright, so many cheerful, earnest young men who are getting ready to take up the work which we must soon expect to lay down. These are the young men who must carry forward humanity in its next step of progress.

The school for the instruction and education of youth in every land is of no less importance than are the tribunals of justice or the provisions for military defense. The end and object of all is the same—the public peace and welfare. The method of obtaining it alone differs. Education of the young is as important a safeguard of the nation as are courts and armies. It is of great moment, then, that we should understand in what true education must consist.

Some one has said that education is that training of men which makes them free. We accept willingly such a definition. True education makes men truly free. True freedom is the power of choosing and selecting at all times that which is best and most profitable. To pos-

sess this power one must know what is best and
then tend towards that alone, leaving aside all
that is less good, however enticing; that is, his
intellect must be trained to know the best and
his will must be trained to choose it. Such
training is true education ; such training makes
men free indeed.

If man is a microcosm, a little universe in
himself, it is evident that true education must
be extended until it provides for all the capa-
bility of the human spirit with all its aptitudes
and natural inclinations. Man is made to the
image and likeness of God. In him shine forth
the perfections of the Divinity, and true education will bring out as much as possible all the
manifestations of that Divinity. In God alone
are all the perfections of Being. Truth, Goodness and Beauty. Perfect human knowledge is
to be acquired only by the study of Him as He
manifests Himself through these perfections in
the created universe.

The sciences study the manifestations of His
being; metaphysics search out the traces of
immutable truth and the relation of created
things to the All-creating intellect; the moral

sciences regard the participation of God's goodness in creation, and, finally, aesthetics con-
template His beauty as found in His works.
Besides, in the human mind exists the faculty
of investigation, by which it proceeds from the
clear knowledge of great first principles to that
of consequences more or less remote. To guide
this process and preserve it from falling into
error we need the science of logic.

But still other faculties and capabilities of
human nature need training that the education
of the whole man may be complete. When we
come to know the perfections of God in the
created universe we naturally desire to describe
them with our words and even to imitate them
in the works of our own hands. Hence the
study of letters and arts. Finally there remains
the practical direction of man's life, private and
social, which is accomplished by the political
and economic sciences. From the outset, therefore, the teacher when instructing and educating
the young must have clearly before his mind
this vast field of learning which is at the dis-
posal of humanity. Let him, therefore, labor
to prepare the minds and hearts of his charges

that they may advance step by step to draw waters from these fountains.

Everything stands between the point from which it started and the end towards which it tends. For man, however, the source from which he has derived all his nature and all his faculties, as well as the one last end towards which he is moving, can be nothing else than the Supreme Intelligence, the Highest Intelligible, since in that alone can he hope to reach the fulness of being, of truth, of good, of beauty, which he finds but in scattered particles in created nature.

Here, then, I would that you should give heed to this consideration, for in it is to be found the strongest argument against atheism and agnosticism on the one hand, and on the other against that system which would attempt the education of youth without illuminating it with the knowledge of the countless relations which man has with God as his beginning and end. And from this same consideration we can easily form a just and wise criterion for judging and deciding on the programme and method of study best adapted and most advantageous—that which promises most for public and private welfare.

And if the Catholic schools of this country differ from the public schools simply in that besides what is taught in the latter, they give the youth a sound moral training and instruct them in the Catholic religion, who will dare to complain of that or call it a defect? Surely the State desires that its youth should not only be instructed in that which it ought to know, but should also be educated in that which it ought to perform; and the State is worthy of all praise in doing all it can to bring about such a result.

But youth, as well as all mankind, has greater and higher needs which cannot be satisfied without a moral and religious education, which cannot be possessed without the aid of those institutions which care especially for moral and religious training. In brief, just as instruction separated from moral education turns out vain and often disastrous, so a moral education without the spirit of religion is a work which makes a man exteriorly moral but not altogether and thoroughly honest.

I would conclude these reflections by remarking:

First, that for these reasons the instruction and education of the young is a work of the highest importance;

Second, that the young should be educated both in mind and heart, according to the constitution of the State, according to the great principles of morality and according to a true religious spirit;

Third, that all good men should co-operate in this great work, so that the American people from generation to generation may remain always safe in its political and social institutions, sincerely honest and faithfully religious.

One who cannot see, or would venture to deny the justice of these considerations would merit no attention from reasonable and well-thinking men.

I have been most happy to accept this reception, and it has given pleasure to the superiors of the institution to offer it to me, since in my unworthiness I have the honor of representing the Holy Father as his delegate. In the midst of the cares of his spiritual government, which extends itself to all the nations of the earth, for the safety and profit of the institutions proper to every one of them, he has no dearer object nor greater joy than in promoting in every possible way the education of the young.

That is the work which he has most warmly
recommended to the Bishops, and to participate
in that work is the greatest and surest title to
his esteem. One might well put into the mouth
of the Holy Father the words of St. John:

" Majorem gratiam non habeo quam ut audiam
filios meos in veritate ambulare. (I have no
greater grace than this, to hear that my children
walk in the truth.) "

I will add that it is well that young men
should have from their earliest days a just idea
of what the Pope is, how lofty his dignity, how
great his authority, how beneficial his actions.
His dignity and his power come directly from
Christ, and the exercise of this power can
only be for the benefit, religious and social,
intellectual and moral, temporal and eternal,
of humanity.

I could not more fittingly conclude than by
expressing this just idea of the Pope in the
words of the illustrious Cardinal Newman, who
beautifully describes what the Pope is viewed
from a social standpoint, just as St. Bernard

beautifully describes him from a theological point of view. Cardinal Newman says:

" Detachment, as we know from spiritual books, is a rare and high Christian virtue. A great saint, St. Philip Neri, said that if he had a dozen really detached men he should be able to convert the world. To be detached is to be loosened from every tie which binds the soul to the earth, to be dependent on nothing sublunary, to lean on nothing temporal ; it is to care simply nothing what other men choose to think or say of us ; to go about our own work because it is our duty, as soldiers go to battle, without a care for the consequences. . . . Now, this detachment is one of the special ecclesiastical virtues of the Popes. They are of all men the most exposed to the temptation of secular connections, and, as history tells us, they have been of all men least subject to it. By their very office they are brought across every form of earthly power, for they have a mission to high as well as low. Under such circumstances any men but they would have a strong leaning towards what is called conservatism, and they have been, and of course are, conservatives in the right sense of the word ;

4

that is, they cannot bear anarchy, they pray for the peace of the world and of all Christian States, and they effectively support the cause of order and good government. The name of religion is but another name for law on the one hand, freedom on the other; and at this very time who are its professed enemies but Socialists, Anarchists and rebels? But a conservative in the political sense of the word commonly signifies something else which the Pope never is and cannot be. It means a man who is at the top of the tree and knows it, and means never to come down, whatever it costs him to keep his place there. It means a man who upholds government and society and the existing state of things, not because it exists, not because it is good and desirable, because it is established, because it is a benefit to the population, because it is full of promise for the future; but rather because he himself is well off in consequence of it, and because to take care of Number One is his main political principle. It means a man who defends religion not for religion's sake, but for the sake of its accidents and externals; and in this sense conservative a Pope can never be, without a simple betrayal of the dispensation committed to him."

Such is the political and social character of a Pope, and such a Pope, if ever one existed, is Leo XIII. In his name, then, and in my own, I thank you for this reception to-night. I thank the Most Reverend Archbishops, the Right Reverend Bishops, the reverend clergy and the gentlemen of the laity for their kindness in showing this respect for my person. I beg the Brothers of the Christian Schools and their pupils to accept my sincerest congratulations and best wishes, and I pray for them the choicest and most abundant divine blessings, and in imploring this blessing for the youth of this renowned institution I ask it for the pupils of all schools of this country under the care of the Brothers, and so feel that I am asking it for the rising hope of the next generation of Americans.

TO THE ALUMNI OF ST. JOHN'S COLLEGE.

In this speech, delivered at the annual banquet of the Alumni, in Washington, D. C., January 31st, 1895, Monsignor Satolli dwells especially upon the way Catholic students should conduct themselves in after life.

It forms a fitting close to the department of Schools and Colleges in our book.

The Most Rev. Delegate said:—

It is a pleasure and an honor to meet this distinguished assemblage of young men who are already well advanced in the course of civil and literary education. Like yourselves, I find three motives for congratulation. In the first place, this custom of meeting at least once a year after you have finished your studies in the schools of the Christian Brothers, is in itself highly praiseworthy; secondly, your intention in holding this annual banquet is to refresh and express anew your gratitude to the Christian Brothers, who have been your affectionate and capable teachers; thirdly, since each step in the young man's life,

52

morally and socially considered, is the result of
the past and the beginning of the future, it is
highly commendable that you should, from your
youth, accustom yourselves to a spirit of polite
and Christian sociability.

Just as, next to the home, come the temple and
the school, so next to the duties to the family
come those to your educators and teachers, who
being called to aid the parent in the important
work of education, have the great task of nourish-
ing and developing the germs of intellectual and
moral life which every man at birth has in his
nature, inserted there by the Supreme Author of
nature and of society. Consequently, to receive
with docility this intellectual light which is
communicated from the teacher to the scholar is
a sign of a fortunate nature and productive of
advantages more appropriate to man than his
very existence.

Early instruction has the greater value during
the tender age at which it is received, because it
is the foundation and preparation for that higher
instruction which is afterwards sought in the
institutions of superior grade. For I believe it
impossible to pursue, with any success, the higher

studies in letters and sciences unless the fundamental instruction has been imparted by careful
method and with good result.   It is your duty to
show in your own selves that the training which
the Christian Brothers give in their wisely
arranged program makes for true culture, and
has its roots in the family, the temple, and the
school.   To have breathed in the course of your
early instruction the pure air of Catholic faith,
while it is a great advantage for yourselves, is
not enough.   A duty lies upon you to show that
you have been aided and strengthened by it for
greater progress in your higher studies.

You are not only in the midst of your families,
but also in social contact with your fellow-citizens.
I find one of the most striking characteristics of
American life to be its sociability.   Indeed one
can scarcely live in this country without feeling
the need of some special association or other; so
that the American people might almost be de-
fined as one grand system of free and friendly
associations looking always to the common weal.
The spirit of mutual good-will and unselfishness
is wonderfully connected with the spirit of private
and social freedom.   Wherefore, the Holy Father

in his recent encyclical has commended this
spirit, the efficacy of which marks the progress
of civilization and assures the common peace.
In this field there is no difference of religious
profession. Nay, even Catholics have the greater
obligation of showing this social spirit and of
bearing themselves toward others with the most
sincere and virtuous good-will. But you should
keep well fixed in your minds that the relations
of the greatest and most extended benevolence
and sociability must ever leave intact the sanctu-
ary of your consciences; and may you never
have the misfortune, for any mistaken purpose
of sociality, to stray from the rectitude of your
religious profession and falsely imagine that in
order to live in harmony it is necessary to give
up those religious differences, which for us are
essential and unchangeable in belief and in
practice. In this regard we must be adamantine;
we must when the occasion offers plainly declare
ourselves; and I am convinced that by so doing
we shall acquire the esteem and respect of our
non-Catholic brethren, who, seeing us sincerely
well-disposed toward them, and at the same time
firm in our religious persuasion, will appreciate

our character, and more easily learn, from our
very firmness and open profession of belief, the
divine character, the truth, and the lovableness
of the Catholic Church. Let us respect those who
are not of our faith, let us exchange with them
all the offices of esteem and friendly feeling, let
us appreciate those virtues and noble qualities
with which Divine Providence has so abundantly
endowed them, who, though not Catholics, yet are
called to come, whenever they choose, and sit at
the banquet of the common Father. We have
our creed, which is not a formula invented by
human wisdom, but through the organ of the
Church received immediately from Christ, just as
our faith and charity together with all our hope
are supernatural gifts from God.

You have undoubtedly learned that there are
four principal sources of human happiness, and
that they are the virtues of prudence, justice,
temperance, and fortitude. By means of these
four virtues all men can, and ought to, labor
together for the common good. Because human
activity depends from reason and free will and
from the peculiar sensitive inclinations, consequently perfect morality requires wisdom of

judgment, rectitude in seeking the good and avoiding the evil, moderation and firmness of temperament, and control of our inclinations that they may not be able to lead us astray nor draw us away from our duty. But the virtues of faith, hope, and charity are the sources of supernatural happiness and the beginning of that blessedness which awaits us in another life. The first four virtues known even to pagan philosophers are simply the expression of the rectitude of the human reason and free will, universal qualities of human nature either in the individual or in the mass. But the other three, being supernatural, are not the product of human reason or will, but free gifts of the eternal wisdom and infinite love of God. It is easy, therefore, to see the impossibility of a combination of different creeds to form an indistinct belief, just as it is absurd to suppose a mean between the affirmation and the denial of one and the same thing. Were we to compare the Catholic belief with any other form of Christianity, we would see that our faith is an integral whole, while the others are but fractions, and differ from ours negatively; so that to be a non-Catholic one but needs to deny some part of our belief, or at least leave it in a state of doubt or in the indifference of mere opinion. The Catholic system is ontological and objective with respect to faith and conscience, just as nature is with respect to science and reason; the system of non-Catholics is subjective and psychological. In every non-Catholic profession divine revelation is held to be contained in the Bible alone, left to the intelligence and acceptance of the reader. But for the Catholic, divine revelation has been immediately communicated to a living organism—that is, to the Church constituted by Christ through the Apostles. Therefore, divine revelation by the inspiration of the sacred writers is found in the Bible, and by the special and continuous assistance of the Holy Ghost in the permanent traditions: and so the inspiration and assistance of the Holy Ghost constitute the objective perennity of Catholic faith. I may then say, with the Italian poet, "You have the new and the old testaments," and these are the common heritage of every Christian profession, and "the Shepherd of the Church who guides you," and this is proper to Catholics.

However, the common desire of all should work in harmony to maintain in the American people the spirit of Christianity, and with few imperceptible exceptions the Government and the people are indeed in harmony on this point, and fully understand that the prevalence of total religious indifferentism would be a great disaster to the commonwealth, no less than if the people were to fall into materialism and atheism. A prominent English writer has said, " The whole matter may, I think, be summed up by saying that Christianity is, in fact, understood to be, though not the legally established religion, yet the national religion. So far from thinking their commonwealth godless, the Americans conceive that the religious character of a government consists in nothing but the religious belief of the individual citizens, and the conformity of their conduct to that belief. They deem the general acceptance of Christianity to be one of the main sources of their national prosperity, and their nation a special object of Divine favor."

Let me express once more my pleasure and satisfaction at being among you to-night; let me congratulate you on the noble record you have already made for yourselves; let me participate in the pride which your old instructors feel in you and in your success; let my few words this evening be to you an encouragement and a guide to future and yet more glorious effort.

PART II.

***

To Catholic Colleges and Schools.

THANKSGIVING DAY SPEECH AT GONZAGA COLLEGE, WASHINGTON, D. C.

A Tribute to Christian Education.

The faculty and students of Gonzaga College, Washington, D. C., gave a reception in honor of Mgr. Satolli, the Apostolic Delegate, in their College hall, on Thanksgiving day, November 30th, 1893.

Several addresses were made, to which Mgr. Satolli responded as follows:—

The whole of America gives thanks to-day to Almighty God, whose kind Providence continues to spread its benefits on this glorious republic.

As all power comes from God, so must we acknowledge as coming from Him, prosperity, the fruit of peace and victory, the fruit of duty performed.

Now, this is the reason why Holy Scripture calls God sometimes the God of Hosts, sometimes the God of peace and charity.

The kingdom of Christ on earth is the greatest manifestation of Divine Providence, and therefore the tribute of gratitude, when offered in the name of Christ, is more acceptable to the Almighty Father, and the prayer offered in Christ's name is more efficacious to obtain ever-increasing benefits for a more and more prosperous future.

Really, we Catholics should be the first both to recognize the benefits of God and to thank Him for them.

Since Catholics should be the most faithful and constant followers of religious and social virtues, so as to be living examples to all who do not share in their faith, they have indeed good reason to be proud and to regard themselves privileged to conform on this day to the President's solemn invitation, and to thank God for protecting and speeding the American republic.

The teachings of St. Paul to the Romans, and the teachings handed down by the early fathers of the church to the faithful, namely, that they should pray constantly for the peace and prosperity of the commonwealth, are the same teachings which the Catholic Church (faithful guardian of ancient traditions) repeats to-day and insists on being observed by her children.

Moreover, we have the important duty as citizens of this republic to show by the sincerity of our actions that we are worthy of enjoying the freedom and prosperity of this noble land.

Hence you, the pupils of the Gonzaga College, could not have selected a more suitable day for a reception to the apostolic delegate than this Thanksgiving day, devoted to a social recognition of God.

Among the Jews and Romans and Greeks no feast was celebrated without the cheerful participation of the young.

The praise and joy radiating from youthful hearts, as well as the grief they show in days of mourning, naturally arouse like sentiments in the hearts of the people.

The offerings of youth seem to be more pleasing to the heavenly throne, bringing thence on earth the graces and favors of God.

In the days of Augustus, the poet Horace composed a hymn, ' Carmen Seculare ' to be sung by the boys and matrons in the streets of Rome,

5

and that is one of the noblest productions of the Muse of Latium.

So your present celebration and songs rise above all other voices, which from every part of the country are directed to heaven in thanksgiving for the past and in prayer for the future.

We may be sure of this, that all Americans (of whatever church they may be members, even if of none) recognize the value of the Catholic school; they are interested in it; they honor it; they wish it to continue and progress: they have learned by experience that children educated in those schools do not fall short in knowledge and in love of the American Constitution; that they do not lag behind the most progressive of the American people; that they are endowed with steadiness of character, with constancy of right purpose; that they are just, active, charitable and generous unto sacrifice.

Such, then, is the magnificent spectacle presented to America by the Catholic schools; not unlike the spectacle given by the first Christians to the whole world in the early centuries of the church. In those days it looked as if pagans and philosophers might despise the faith, and calumniate the customs and religion of the Christians, but in reality they could not conceal very long their true judgment, nor hide their astonishment at the spectacle of the social and religious virtues preached by Christians.

If they had favored the new religion instead of persecuting it, how advantageous it would have been for the public welfare. If, on the one hand, they had also recognized and fostered harmony between Christian truth and morality, and, on the other hand, the spirit of social and public life, how much better it would have been for themselves and for the Church.

It was impossible at the time to bring about this harmony, because the civil constitution of those days was imbued with errors and superstitions, and because, with no good reason, it was believed that ruin of the state would inevitably follow the disappearance of those superstitions.

But thanks be to God, and glory to the men who inspired the American Constitution, such a state of things as obtained in Rome is not possible here.

And I will say that whoever seriously meditates on the principles of the American Constitution,

or is acquainted with the present conditions of
the American republic, cannot deny that the influence and action of Catholic faith and morality
is favorable in every way to the letter and spirit
of the American Constitution.

For the more public opinion and the government approve the Catholic schools, the more
will the welfare of the commonwealth be
advanced.

Catholic education is a very sure safeguard for
the permanence throughout the centuries of the
Constitution, and an enlightened guide of the
Republic in civil progress. From this source
will come that assimilation so necessary in a
land made up of many elements, for the perfect
organization of that great progressive body, the
American republic.

Behold the sincere expression of my conviction,
and, so to speak, the profession of my faith in this
matter.

Did I speak differently I should be unfaithful
to my mission, ungrateful to the generous hospitality which I have enjoyed and am enjoying in
America; and, moreover, I should have given
the lie to my first and unchangeable convictions.

Every Catholic school is a safe guardian of youth, and it is at the same time a place of training for the American youth where they are brought up for the good of church and country.

Heaven grant that the Catholic schools may continue.

May they increase in numbers, and grow stronger.

May they reach the highest perfection and be enriched with the blessings of God, deserving of the commendation of the Church and the Holy Father, and be honored and appreciated by every honest citizen, from the illustrious President down to the most humble workman.

Their enemies are they who know them not, and who are not animated by the spirit of the Church, but are lacking in the sentiments of true liberty.

This college of St. Aloysius well deserves to be situated at the seat of the federal government, resting, as it were, beneath the shadow of the Capitol.

Young men, before you is the great and noble array of those who have gone before you, and who are to-day able and honored citizens. Follow, then, their example; devote yourselves, mind and heart, to the lessons that are here imparted to you, and you will certainly become a worthy generation of Aloysian alumni, a band of noble and honorable citizens.

May then, Heaven bless you, and I, as the humble representative of the Holy Father, I bless you from all my heart.

While at Waterbury, Conn., on May 15th, 1894, His Excellency, accompanied by Mayor Kilduff, the V. Rev. John Mulcahy, V. G., and the Rev. Father Bandini, paid a visit to the High School.

After a most courteous reception by Superintendent Crosby and the teachers, Mgr. Satolli delivered the following address :—

On arriving in your city I received a cordial invitation to visit your public schools. Cheerfully have I come here, and in meeting the Superintendent, the teachers and the board of education, do I feel highly honored.

For more than twenty years of my life, my principal occupation was that of teaching. Humanities first claimed my care, then philosophy and afterwards theology. The happiness of those days endeared that office of teaching to me. Gladly should I have continued in it, had it been in my power.

It is natural, then, that it should be gratifying

71

to me to visit schools and find myself again
amongst teachers and pupils.

My intimate conviction is, that the position of
a teacher is the noblest of all, as it is the most
useful and necessary.

The history of the origin and progress of the
schools of a nation is a compendium of the history
of that nation.

The great Athenian philosopher, Aristotle,
teaches that there are three institutions necessary
to the welfare of every nation, namely, the civil,
the military, and the educational, three institutions that are intimately connected and inter-
dependent, but of them, education should hold
the place of honor, as upon it the others depend.

Let me add that the industrial, agricultural
and mechanical arts would not flourish nor give
the benefits which society requires, unless they
were preceded and accompanied by a certain
amount of education.

You have visible evidences of this fact in this
country, wherein industrial, agricultural and
mechanical arts have reached their highest development; and this is the result of the wonderful diffusion of education.

It pleases me much to know that we are of the same opinion with regard to the necessity for the school to educate the whole man. I mean by this, the training of the intellect and heart, not only that he may know nature and provide what is useful and necessary for life, but also, that he may live as an honest, upright citizen, possessing all the moral virtues that should adorn a man.

As the gymnasium is necessary to develop the physical man, so it is needful to practice religion in order to strengthen and nourish the soul, and to make the man just and charitable. This moral education, so necessary, must be animated by the Divine spirit.

To say that the Constitution of the United States forbids the civil power to frame laws about religion, or to become involved in matters strictly pertaining to religion, is one thing. But it is altogether different to hold that the American Constitution is godless, or that the American life requires not the influence of religion. For it is consonant with the spirit of true liberty and well-ordered government, so to educate youth and so to enlighten their minds that they may not only know true religion, but also, love and practice it.

The youth of ancient Greece entered the lists on Mount Olympus, and so much importance was attached to their athletic exhibitions that periods of time were designated as the Olympiades.

The youth of the Roman republic spent their lives in military pursuits in the camp of Mars, but American youth spend their time in the school-room, to form a nation eminently free and desirous of peace and prosperity.

The state has every reason to put forth its zeal for the advancement of the public schools. It deserves great praise for having surmounted so many obstacles; for having erected so many schools, and for the excellent discipline maintained in them. Because all this tends to build up the character of American youth, as well as to exclude anything prejudicial to their moral and religious interests.

Since fixing my residence in Washington, I have walked daily through its spacious avenues, and passing by, I am pleased to see on every side, great buildings devoted to primary and higher education. What important and effective agencies they must be.

It is my sincere wish that they will persevere and ever go on to nobler, higher things.

All within its power the state does, and beyond doubt, encourages all institutions built upon the American spirit.

For such are in harmony with the school system, as by law established, a system whose object is to protect and assure a moral and religious education. And these institutions are Catholic schools.

In the domain of instruction and education, church and state go hand in hand, working together to accomplish the noble purpose of forming citizens worthy of this country, and sincere believers in the Catholic religion.

The state, in so far as it is free and progressive, need fear nothing from the Catholic Church, but on the contrary, ought to expect great benefit from it.

Because it was her institutions and effective influence that broke the shackles of slavery, and secured true civil and Christian liberty, and produced modern civilization from out of the confusion of barbarism.

Accept, then, ladies and gentlemen, the expression of my gratitude for your kind invitation
and my admiration of the prosperity so evident
in your city.

It is my sincere wish that the common welfare
will be promoted by your schools and your city.

———

SPEECH AT ST. JOHN'S COLLEGE, WASHINGTON, D. C.

The occasion of the delivery of the following address on Christian education was a brilliant one.

In it the Apostolic Delegate briefly exposes some of the debts we, of the present age, owe to the Papacy, and its consistent educational policy from the beginning.

He also gives a well-deserved tribute of praise to that noble teaching order of the Church, the Christian Brothers.

On Washington's Birthday, 1894, and in Washington's city, the faculty, students and Alumni Society of St. John's College, conducted by the Christian Brothers, gave a reception in honor of the Apostolic Delegate.

A distinguished audience of Congressmen, Army and Naval officers, and members of the Diplomatic corps, was present.

Addresses of welcome were made by Brother Fabrician, president of the College, Hon. Bourke Cochran and others.

Mgr. Satolli responded as follows: —

Permit me to express my utmost satisfaction and sincere gratification for these musical and literary exercises.

These exercises, it seems to me, are not so much in my own honor as they are a testimonial of filial respect and devotedness to our Holy Father, who has just completed the festive year of his episcopal jubilee.

Ever since the triumphal entry of Christ into the city of Jerusalem, when the children cried out, " Hosannah to the Son of David : Blessed is he that cometh in the name of the Lord," Christian people have been accustomed to employ youthful voices in the celebration of religious festivities.

All nations which aspire by means of free institutions and the development of human industries to a high degree of civilization and refinement, revere the name of the Holy Father. For, treading in the footsteps of his Divine Master, who is the Prince of Peace, the Pope always has been the zealous advocate of justice, the source of prosperity and happiness.

I am also glad of this opportunity to testify my appreciation of an institution, which among the many engaged in the training of American youth, is one of the most flourishing. In devoting themselves to their noble task, the teachers of this College are carrying out the idea of their holy founder. Like Ignatius of Loyola, Joseph

Calasanctius, Jerome Æmiliani and Vincent de
Paul, the Blessed La Salle lives in the army of
wise and virtuous Christian Brothers, to whom is
entrusted the mission of gathering children under
the mantle of charity, there to nourish them by
their zealous instructions.

Thus the Church, in compliance with the
requirements of times and circumstances, guarantees a succession of worthy members by
tenderly nurturing her children in the happiest
period of their lives.

It is universally acknowledged that the Blessed
La Salle selected the kind of education which
was best suited to the circumstances and environ-
ments of the people for whose benefit he had
sacrificed so much.

His system of education is found to be most
suitable here in America, and is that which is
followed by nearly all schools, whether private or
public. Thus it is that the sons of La Salle are
equally at home in Rome, in Paris, or in Washington. Statesmen and wise educators have
always held it to be of the greatest importance,
not only that large and well-equipped school
buildings be erected, but also that capable and

painstaking teachers, well trained in pedagogic methods, having well conceived standards, should perform the important task of forming the heart and training the intellect of youth.

To such a work the Fathers of the Church did not disdain to give their serious attention; for this purpose they composed books on pedagogy which even now are worthy of the admiration of our eminent educators.

Listen to what St. John Chrysostom says on education :—

"Omni certe pictore, omni certe statuario, ceterisque ejusmodi omnibus excellentiorem hunc duco, qui juvenum animos fingere non ignorat."

"What nobler than to direct the minds and to form the hearts of the young? The man who understands the art of governing the souls of youth, appears to me to be more excellent than the painter, the sculptor, or the most skillful artist."

This is why the Bishops of the entire Catholic world, as well as the Popes, have always endeavored to co-operate with the civil authorities. Yea, more, even to urge them on to noble activity in building schools, and founding institutions, where the youth of the humblest as well as the most aristocratic classes would be gathered together for the benefit of Church and State alike.

Notwithstanding all that the enemies of the Papacy and the Church may say, there is no fact more certain in the long history of twenty centuries, than that the Popes, with a holy zeal superior, or at least equal, to that of the most eminent statesmen and philanthropists of all time, have employed their ability and their wealth in furthering the education of the young and the advancement of Christian civilization.

Let me add that the inspiring genius of Catholicity in the field of education has ever been associated with the genius of the greatest legislators and civilizers, while at the same time the institutions of the Church have never opposed the useful and beneficial institutions inaugurated by the civil power.

Both have always been in friendly accord, and have given to each other friendly assistance.

Catholicity, now as ever, keeps abreast with the highest civilization.

You have but to glance at the Chicago exhibition, the quadro-centennial of the achievement

6

of an Italian and a Catholic, who brought with
him in his small caravel the germ of civilization
from Europe to this newly discovered country.

That exhibition has shown how wonderfully
harmonized are the civil and social elements, the
arts and the sciences, religion and civilization,
Catholic education and civil progress—in a word,
how well material prosperity can combine with
the moral and religious life of a people.

The educational exhibit of Catholic schools was
acknowledged by all to be most creditable.

We may feel assured that America will not
easily forget that feature of the World's Fair.

It is my belief that the future of the educational
question in the United States will show the happy
result of that exhibit. over which presided a wise
and gentle Brother, a son of La Salle.

Again, I have observed in many countries that
the faithful care exercised by the Christian
Brothers over the moral and religious education
of their charges, has kept even pace with the
best educational standard established by the civil
authorities in the several countries where they are.

Therefore. both the Church and the State,
especially here in America. look upon the Chris-

tian Brothers as cultivators of a precious mission in the field of popular education.

Thus it is that the young men leaving their schools are filled with the most flattering hopes, and show themselves exuberant with youthful energy, proving themselves honest and strong in the profession of their faith, just, charitable, generous and courageous citizens.

In conclusion, as a faithful interpreter of the affectionate intentions of the Holy Father towards educational institutions, especially toward those of the Christian Brothers, I am happy to pay this tribute of admiration and praise, while I implore the choicest blessings of Almighty God upon all of you.

SPEECH AT EPIPHANY APOSTOLIC COLLEGE.

On the Feast of the Epiphany, January 6th, 1893, the titular feast of the Epiphany Apostolic College, Highland Park, Baltimore, Md., Mgr. Satolli attended a dramatic entertainment in the play hall of that institution, at which His Eminence, James Cardinal Gibbons, and the late Bishop O'Farrell, with his Vicar-general, Dr. McFaul, now the ordinary of the Trenton diocese, were also present. When the curtain had dropped on the last act, His Excellency arose and spoke as follows:

Your Eminence. Right Reverend Bishop, Very Reverend and Reverend Fathers. and Students:—

Sitting here my thoughts transported me to another clime, for just one year ago to-day I saw similar scenes in my own native land. Although the speech in which the players have spoken is as yet unfamilar to me, yet the action of the piece had a language all its own. and easily by voice and gesture have I understood what is intended by the drama.

84

I thank you all for this entertainment. Looking forward into the years I see that you students, with the help of Him who died to save us all, will work in Christ's vineyard, as eagerly and as ardently as you have worked to-day.

The mission to which you are called is a high, a noble one: an apostolic vocation is given to you. The work you would engage in is one requiring combined efforts.

To-day in all truth can we say of the black people of America:—"The harvest truly is great, but the laborers are few."

The Church has been asking the Lord of the Harvest to send forth His laborers, and you, young gentlemen. have been chosen to labor. You may never be able to bring the Negroes wholly, as a people, to the Holy Catholic Church, but I know that He Whose call you have heard and obeyed will bless the labors of the priests of this Congregation. And why? Because Our Lord loves the poor, the lowly, and for such as are animated with His spirit, He has laid up treasures that no man can steal.

While here, my dear students, you must cultivate the spirit of prayer, the spirit that raises man to see as God sees, that makes him think and feel as He thought and felt while He walked on earth " continually doing good."

Be subject also to those who are set over you. for the obedient man shall speak of victories.

Leaving your kinsfolk, your homes with all their tender ties, you have come here to fit your-selves for the highest mission given by God to man. You would be instruments to proclaim the marvellous love of God, to tell to a benighted people the story of Him, Who was the chief actor in the drama of Calvary.

You would be ministers of the Catholic Church. priests of God, and devoted to your fellow men. Here you have come, and here you study. How do you study? Or, perhaps I should tell you since I myself have had somewhat to do with teaching. How must you proceed? Be diligent; they alone who understand what they read, who apply themselves with earnest endeavor, who follow the maxim of Horace, " Nocturna versate manu, versate diurna," are the men who become proficient in human, as well as in divine, science.

This age, if you will read the signs of the times, demands men of learning, men who are capable of rendering a reason for the faith that is in them, who are up. in a word, with the ever-flowing tide of modern advancement.

The main difficulty with most young men who study as you do, is that they have no patience, or at best, only little of this admirable virtue. They do not get along fast enough and are apt to become fretful and peevish. They forget that the best of works have been of slow growth.

Continents have not risen in a day. Catholic doctrine has not attained its present form within this century. No! all of these, and more, have been the labor of many, many years. So it is with studies. And I believe that as you advance on the pathway of knowledge you will learn how to curb the desire that hurries onward, knowing not whither it goes. But as in the spiritual life, so in the student's College life. You must have perseverance. Go on, look not backward. press forward, keep ever before you the end you would attain. Pray for light. Veni, Sancte Spiritus is a prayer for all, but surely it is the special prayer of ecclesiastical students.

Use it frequently, as did St. Thomas; ask her, the "Sedes Sapientiae," for help and counsel.

And may the spirit of the Doctor of the Schools be among you, may the love of the Mother of God be with you, may God bless you in your present labor, may He prosper the works of your hands when, as His anointed ones, you go to toil for the salvation of those souls who "sit in darkness and in the shadow of death."

Archbishop Satolli visited St. Charles' College, Ellicott City, Md., November 4th, 1892. The reception given to His Excellency was most enthusiastic.

To the Latin address of welcome, the Delegate responded in substance as follows:—

Literary studies are all important, in the first place, as a means of civilization. With their cultivation, progress goes hand in hand; with their neglect, progress ceases. Literary studies, again, develop to its full capacity the intellect, which, though inorganic, must draw its knowledge from imagination and sense. A mind thus prepared, will take up with pleasure and profit the higher studies of philosophy and theology. But the priest must not be merely a student. He has a mission among men; he must teach them to know the truth, to love the good, to appreciate the beautiful, and this power of appreciation cannot better be cultivated than by a diligent study of what is rightly termed belles-lettres.

89

———

The students of Loyola College, Baltimore, gave an impromptu reception to Monsignor Satolli and his suite, Monsignori Sbaretti and Papi, on April 16th, 1894.

He was heartily welcomed by the students. Father Brady, prefect of studies, spoke in behalf of the faculty.

Mgr. Satolli responded in English, thanking them for their greeting. He expressed his happiness at meeting them.

He was always glad to meet young men—particularly students.

They were the hope of the family, the State and the Church. So much depended upon them that their education was a matter of prime solicitude.

He reminded them that no education could be true which separated instruction in letters, sciences and arts from religion and morality. He hoped the students fully valued this privilege, for they were providentially favored in having for instructors those whose system was based on this important principle.

90

THE HARMONY OF CHURCH AND STATE.

In June, 1894, Mgr. Satolli celebrated Pontifical Mass in St. Patrick's Cathedral, New York.

The occasion was the Golden Jubilee of the League of the Sacred Heart attached to that beautiful Basilica.

The work of the Catholic Summer School was brought to the attention of the Delegate Apostolic by the Rev. Joseph H. McMahon, who is the chairman of its executive committee, as well as Director of the League.

Mgr. Satolli listened attentively to the explanation of its objects and methods.

Then, blessing the work, he said :—

From the experience that I have gathered in America, I do believe that it is the country of all others in which Catholic truth may have the largest field of action.

We only need freedom of speech, and that is most ample in America. But the exposition of truth must be clear and plain. I regret that sometimes the truth has been set forth incompletely. Truth possesses in itself the power to reach the intellect; it needs only to be presented clearly and entirely. It will then be accepted not only by Catholics, but also by Protestants and infidels.

I mean by those who are outside the pale of the Church, by reason of their honest conviction, not on account of systematic opposition, prejudice or bigotry.

Those who are influenced by these latter motives, are many centuries behind modern progress.

And I would be very much pleased to see the Catholic Summer School incorporate with its objects, another point of very great importance, namely, the presentation to the American people of the precise idea of the relations between the Church and the State. They should show the inevitable existing harmony between these two institutions.

This is much to be desired and will be fruitful of good.

In this matter I find a surprising want of knowledge in America. I am speaking about what is commonly called public ecclesiastical law, which precisely deals with the fundamental, or rather, the essential constitution of the Church and the State, and determines the limits of action of both authorities in such a way as to prevent the conflicts that unfortunately disturb social peace and retard social progress.

SPEECH AT ST. BONAVENTURE'S COLLEGE, ALLEGANY, CATTARAUGUS CO., N. Y.

The Franciscan Fathers at the above place entertained the Apostolic Delegate for two days in June, 1894. There were ordinations and dedications.

The Delegate arrived on a special train by the Erie Railway, and was greeted with music furnished by the College band, and escorted through triumphal arches made of roses and adorned with United States flags.

Numerous speeches, original poems and addresses of welcome were made in Latin, Italian, English, French, German and Spanish, to which Mgr. Satolli responded in substance:—

That he had heard much of Allegany Franciscan hospitality, but that which he had heard was by no means commensurate with what he had experienced; that he had visited many educational institutions in America, and had unfailingly experienced great pleasure in so doing, but never did he feel more intense satisfaction than that afforded him by the general manifestation of undying fidelity to Faith and Fatherland, dis-

94

played on the occasion by the students and faculty of St. Bonaventure's.

He congratulated Bishop Ryan on having in his diocese such a noble Catholic institution, and said, that though it always afforded him a peculiar pleasure to come to the diocese of Buffalo, yet his satisfaction would be thenceforward materially enhanced, owing to his acquaintance with Allegany.

St. Bonaventure's, he continued, deserves a prominent place among the institutions of the land. He concluded by hoping that the clergy would continue, by every possible means, to second the efforts made by the sons of St. Francis in the cause of religion, education and patriotism.

PART III.

The Relations of Church and State.

THE RELATIONS OF CHURCH AND STATE.

In this address, delivered at the annual banquet of the Carroll Institute, Washington, D. C., Feb. 26th, 1895, His Excellency, the Apostolic Delegate, shows that the State has nothing to fear, but everything to hope from the existence of the Catholic Church in her midst. He reviews the recent encyclical of the Holy Father, and points out that, "there is nothing to fear, but everything to hope in the instruction and education given by the Church, to Catholic youth. Beneficent societies, the freedom of the press, the freedom of religion, have nothing to fear from the Church."

The address was a response to the toast, "His Holiness, the Pope," and was read by Mgr. Satolli's secretary, Rev. Dr. Rooker:—

It is now two years since the Carroll Institute entered this new building, and I remember with great pleasure the reception so kindly given to me on that occasion. It is a satisfaction to me to recall that what I then said concerning the Pope and America, was in perfect harmony with what the Holy Father himself has just expressed in his recent encyclical, which will ever remain

an imperishable monument in the history of the
American Church and nation. (See *infra*, Part
IX.) It is the duty of whoever receives a
public mission, to conform himself in word and
act to the intention and desires of the one who
sends him, and I have the gratifying consciousness of having acted in conformity with the
intention and desires of the Holy Father, thus
far, in the exercise of my office as his delegate in
America. For this reason I await fearlessly the
judgment of the public and of posterity. Justice,
charity, and loyalty to Church and country are
always and everywhere, true characteristics of
Papal diplomacy. I dare affirm that the Papal
encyclical is a complete and authoritative syn-
thesis of all that I have had occasion to express
from the beginning up to the present moment.
In fact, the Holy Father begins his encyclical by
indicating his esteem and affection for the
American people: " We highly esteem and love
exceedingly the young and vigorous American nation, in which we plainly discern latent
forces for the advancement, alike of civilization
and of Christianity." Then he shows the close
relations which exist between the Catholic Church

and the American Republic, bestowing highest praise on the immortal founder of that republic. He sees the first reason for this close relation in the fact that the discoverer of America brought with him to these shores the Christian faith and the spirit of Catholicism, and just as he carried with him in his ships, "as well the germs of mighty states as the principles of the Catholic religion," so in his person the Catholic Church came to imprint the sign of life on the brow of the American people. Next, the Pope sees a reason for the intimacy between the Church and this people in the coincidence by which at the same moment this nation won and fixed its independence and the Catholic hierarchy was founded here, for, "at the very time when the popular suffrage placed the great Washington at the helm of the republic, the first Bishop was set by apostolic authority over the American Church." And, he adds, "the well-known friendship and familiar intercourse which subsisted between these two men seems to be an evidence that the United States ought to be conjoined in concord and amity with the Catholic Church." From the fact, the Holy Father rises to the theoretic consideration of the reason, comparing the nature of a free government with the spirit of the Catholic Church, and saying, "Without morality the state cannot endure, a truth which that illustrious citizen of yours whom we have just named, with a keenness of insight worthy of his genius and statesmanship, perceived and proclaimed. But the best and strongest support of morality is religion. She, by her very nature, guards and defends all the principles on which duties are founded, and, setting before us the motives most powerful to influence us, commands us to live virtuously and not transgress. Now, what is the Church other than a legitimate society, founded by the will and ordinance of Jesus Christ, for the preservation of morality and the defence of religion?"

Having started simultaneously, so to speak, the Holy Father finds natural the simultaneous progress and development of the nation and the Church. He says: "That your republic is progressing and developing by giant strides is patent to all; and this holds good in religious matters also. For even as your cities, in the course of one century, have made a marvelous increase in wealth and power, so do we behold the Church from scant and slender beginnings grown with rapidity to be great and exceedingly flourishing."

In consequence, no wise man can doubt that the future destiny of this great Republic must remain associated with the fortunes which attend the Church *una sors feret utrumque.* The Pope says: "All intelligent men are agreed, and we ourselves have with pleasure intimated it above, that America seems destined for greater things. Now, it is our wish that the Catholic Church should not only share in, but help to bring about, this prospective greatness. We deem it right and proper that she should, by availing herself of the opportunities daily presented to her, keep equal step with the Republic in the march of improvement, at the same time striving to the utmost, by her virtue and her institutions, to aid in the rapid growth of the States."

From these considerations it is easy to see how Catholics should live and act in order that their influence may be exercised for the greatest good of the nation. "Wherefore, we ardently desire that this truth should sink day by day more deeply into the minds of Catholics, namely, that

they can in no better way, safeguard their individual interests and the common good than by
yielding a hearty submission and obedience to
the Church." By these words Leo XIII does
nothing else than repeat the social lessons taught
by SS. Peter and Paul in their epistles to Christians of all ages. Moreover, the Holy Father
recalls the teaching of his former encyclicals, and
wishes that the Christian doctrine, so clearly set
forth in them, should be preached by the clergy
and constantly recommended to the practice of
the faithful. " Let those of the clergy, therefore,
who are occupied with the instruction of the
multitude, treat plainly this topic of the duties of
citizens, so that all may understand and feel the
necessity in political life of conscientiousness,
self-restraint, and integrity; for that cannot be
lawful in public, which is unlawful in private
affairs. On this whole subject there are to be
found, as you know, in the encyclical letters
written by us from time to time in the course of
our Pontificate, many things which Catholics
should attend to and observe. In these writings
and expositions we have treated of human liberty,
of the chief Christian duties, of civil government,

and of the Christian constitution of States, draw-
ing our principles as well from the teaching of
the Gospels, as from reason. They, then, who
wish to be good citizens and to discharge their
duties faithfully, may readily learn from our
letters the ideal of an upright life. In like
manner, let the priests be persistent in keeping
before the minds of the people the enactments of
the Third Council of Baltimore, particularly
those which inculcate the virtue of temperance,
the frequent use of the sacraments, and the
observance of the just laws and institutions of
the Republic."

In special manner, the Holy Father recom-
mends societies and associations as of great
service to the welfare of the people, and gives
the general rules to be observed concerning them,
that religion may be safeguarded, and the peace
of society at large be protected. As Christ intended to renew the moral world in all its forms
of life, private, domestic, and civil; as Christ intended to render Christian, the individual, the
family, and the entire nation; so the Church has
always been the fruitful mother of social institutions for every art and trade, and for every kind

of private and public beneficence. But such associations should be organs of usefulness never separated from justice and honesty. This is the only criterion by which the Church judges, approves, or disapproves any association.

Another great and powerful factor in the development of the nation whose importance the Pope fully recognizes is the press, and with profound wisdom he lays down certain general rules, which, if observed, will prevent any damage arising from the abuse of this remarkable power. He says, "We are aware that already there labor in this field many men of skill and experience, whose diligence demands words of praise rather than of encouragement. Nevertheless, since the thirst for reading and knowledge is so vehement and widespread amongst you, and since, according to circumstances, it can be productive of either good or evil, every effort should be made to increase the number of intelligent and well-disposed writers, who take religion for their guide and virtue for their constant companion." No one can fail to see how wise are the admonitions he gives the Catholic press. He encourages its existence, secures its liberty, and protects it from error.

The great mass of non-Catholics in this country have willingly received the words addressed to them in the encyclical, and have understood that the Holy Father recognizes their goodness of heart and kindly dispositions, which fit them so well for knowing and embracing the truth. He exhorts the Catholic clergy and laity to use toward their non-Catholic brethren that kindness and charity which is the very soul of their own religion, and to draw them to the truth and to the unity of faith in the bond of charity by the example of their virtuous lives.

Broad and complete is the demonstration given by the Holy Father in this encyclical that the state has nothing to fear but everything to hope from the existence of the Catholic Church in her midst. She has everything to hope and nothing to fear, not only as regards her independence and constitutional liberty, but as regards the liberty of political parties as well, to none of which does the Church or the Pope desire that Catholic interests should bind themselves. The Church holds herself on a higher plane and looks only to the common good, to the reign of truth, justice, and peace. There is nothing to

fear, but everything to hope in the instruction
and education given by the Church to Catholic
youth.   Beneficent societies, the freedom of the
press, the freedom of religion, have nothing to
fear from the Church. Wherefore, after this magnificent exposition of Catholic truth in the recent
encyclical, all sinister pre-occupations concerning
the possibility or impossibility of a true harmony
between Catholic spirit and civil and political
liberty should disappear.   One of the Church's
teachings is that a popular form of government
is a just and proper one.   It has never happened
that the Church or a Pope entered. of his own
accord, into the vast field of civil government ; but
history sufficiently proves that trouble has always
arisen when governments have overstepped the
limits of their legitimate authority, and have
sought to interfere in religious matters.   The
danger of such trouble does not exist in this
country, as is evident from the spirit of the
Constitution and from the loyalty of those who
are its custodians.   To them does it belong to
maintain the spirit of the Constitution in pro-
hibiting the framing of any law in matters of
religion, and the using of any distinction among

the people based on religious differences; but, it is certainly against the spirit of the Constitution to refuse the co-operation offered by Catholic institutions, or to exclude them solely because they are Catholic.

There are those who think that only now, under the rule of Leo XIII, has the Church become the friend of popular government; but this is not so. The Catholic Church, always taking count of the difference of social conditions in various times and places, has ever shown a particular sympathy for popular government. A distinguished writer says, "That the pages of history testify to the close relationship existing between popular governments and the Catholic faith, is shown by the fact that all republics since the Christian era have sprung into existence under the influence of the Catholic Church, were founded in ages of faith, and by a Catholic people. The republic of San Marino has existed in an entirely Catholic population in the heart of Italy one thousand years or more, and that of Andorra, on the borders of Spain and France, has stood the same number of years; but these republics are small in numbers and in extent of territory. Grant it;

yet they are large enough, and have existed long enough to illustrate the principle that republicanism is congenial with the Catholic religion, and at home in a Catholic population. Then, again, we have the Italian republics in Catholic ages—those of Venice, Pisa, Milan, Florence, Padua, Bologna. In fact, there were no less than two hundred republics spread over the fair land of Italy. The principal Italian cities may be regarded as model republics. Some were founded in the ninth, others in the tenth or eleventh century, and lasted several hundred years. Venice stood one thousand years and more. The Swiss republic was founded in mediæval times, and counts among its heroes and martyrs of political liberty, William Tell and Arnold von Winkelried, both of whom were faithful sons of the Catholic Church. How can we explain that the love of liberty and popular institutions should thus spring up spontaneously and exclusively on Catholic soil, unless it be that republicanism and Catholicity have one common root?"

I cannot conclude without calling your attention to one other important consideration concerning the relation of the Church to the nation

in this country. The opinion is certainly growing, that we are nearing a most critical point in
history, and that in this country especially great
problems will soon demand positive solution.
All the horrors of a social revolution are pre-
dicted by men no less renowned for accurate and
calm thinking than Prof. Goldwin Smith and
Prof. Von Holst. All agree in selecting this
country as the field of the greatest of the dis-
orders which threaten society. This being so, it
is interesting to note the words of a non-Catholic
writer in the latest number of an important maga-
zine. He says: "The tacit acknowledgment of
the religious primacy of the successor of St.
Peter is one of the clearest signs of the times.
It is a significant recognition of the fact that
the Catholic Church holds the solution of the
terrible problem which lies on the threshold of
the twentieth century, and that it belongs to the
Pope alone to pronounce our social *pax vobiscum*."

PART IV.

Temperance.

ON TEMPERANCE.

Outside of the School Question, few steps in the busy life of the Delegate Apostolic, since he came to us, have excited more general attention among all classes of Americans, irrespective of religious creeds, than his attitude on the Temperance Question.

We shall give a brief account of the matter.

The Rt. Rev. John Ambrose Watterson, D. D., Bishop of Columbus, Ohio, addressed a circular letter to his clergy, under date of March 1st, 1894. After stating the necessity of practising temperance, and earnestly appealing in behalf of total abstinence, giving incontrovertible arguments in favor of both, the Bishop laid down the rules of action to be followed by the Catholic societies and the clergy in the matter. To quote his own widely read and stirring words:—

"To give greater efficacy, both to the recommendations of the bishops, and to the declarations of our Catholic laity at the recent Congress in Chicago, concerning the saloon business, I hereby withdraw my approbation from any and every Catholic society, or branch or division thereof in this diocese, that has a liquor dealer or saloon keeper at its head or anywhere among its officers; and I suspend every such society itself from its rank and privilege as a Catholic society, until it ceases

115

to be so officered.   Happily, there is not much occasion now for
such suspensions.   I again publish the condition, without which
for some years past, I have declined to approve of new societies
or new branches of old organizations in this diocese, namely :

"'That no one who is engaged either as principal or agent in
the manufacture or sale of intoxicating liquors can be admitted
to membership.'

" I do not hereby condemn the liquor business in itself; but
my motive in these restrictions is to promote the dignity and
honor, and increase the influence and usefulness of our Catholic societies, and to remove from them and from ourselves the
reproach that has too often attached to them and us, even to
the detriment of religion, both on account of the saloon business itself and the manner in which it is usually carried on.

" In regard to societies that have been long established in
the diocese, and which have obligations of justice to their existing members because of what are called benefit and insurance
features, I do not wish to interfere with the standing and
claims of present members on this score; but I insist on the
condition already mentioned for new societies, as an essential
rule and norma for the admission of new members into old
societies from this time forward.

" You will make this rule known to the organizations in
your parish and have it faithfully observed.   It is sure, however, to commend itself to every right-spirited and healthy
association of Catholic gentlemen.

" Be kind enough to take a personal interest in your societies.   They look for counsel and encouragement from you, and
your efforts in their behalf will not be unrewarded.   You will

have greater comfort from them; for, as a rule, they consist of well-meaning, faithful and earnest men, who are grateful for the sympathetic and tactful efforts of their pastor for their welfare, and may become valuable auxiliaries to him in many important ways. Encourage them also to be abstemious both for their own temporal and eternal good, and as an example to others.

"If there are saloon-keepers in your parish, who call themselves Catholics, and yet carry on their business in a forbidden and disedifying way, or sell on Sundays either openly or under any sort of guise or disguise in violation of the civil law and to the hurt of order and religion, and the scandal of any part of the community, you will refuse them absolution, should they perchance come to receive the Sacraments, unless they resolve and promise to cease offending in these or other ways, and to conduct their business blamelessly, if they can, or get out of it and keep out of it altogether. Their case is to be treated then and afterwards like any other relatively proximate occasion of sin."

As the Bishop ordered this letter read in all the churches twice during the season of Lent, its provisions became well known and many were inclined to carp at it, particularly was this the case with those engaged in the liquor business, for it was a severe blow at their interests.

Certain Catholic societies felt much aggrieved at the action of the Bishop, considering it a severe and unjust curtailment of their liberties. A protest and an appeal were formulated and addressed to the Apostolic Delegate at Washington, who, in the course of a few weeks, replied as follows: —

March 15, 1894.

Dear Sir:—I received in due time your letter
of the 24th of February, and have given the
matter referred to therein my earliest consideration. I have carefully examined your case, and
after doing so, I am glad to be able to say, that
the action of the Rt. Rev. Bishop towards your
society, has been such as to prove how well the
Bishop is animated towards the same, and that
in all this affair he has looked for nothing but
the good of religion and your society.

In giving his directions, the Bishop has not
been led by any motive of personal feeling, but
only by the desire of the good of the society, and
of religion, the interests of which he has the right
and duty to protect among all his subjects.

Furthermore, the Association as Catholic, not
only should not oppose the Bishop's action, but
it also ought to co-operate with him in order to
bring about in the best way the society's welfare.
It is certain, that only by showing a complete
obedience to the Bishop's orders, your association
will be able to deserve the name of Catholic, a
title of which your society is justly proud, and to

enjoy at the same time all the privileges which are accorded by ecclesiastical authority to Catholic societies.

I hope, therefore, that your society will not hesitate to show the deference due to the Bishop by conforming to his directions regarding the election of officers, and the way of holding the entertainments of the association.

I have no doubt that the society, which is anxious to look for the spiritual, no less than the temporal welfare of its members, will appreciate my advice and regulate itself according to the same; and thus its prosperity will always tend to grow more and more to its own benefit and that of religion.

FRANCIS, ARCHBISHOP SATOLLI,
Apostolic Delegate.

As clear-cut as this letter was, it was not satisfactory, and it was hoped that the Apostolic Delegate's appearance in Columbus would cause him to modify, at least in part, his endorsement of the Bishop's action.

Another petition, more general in character, and signed by a number of members of Catholic Societies and others, was drawn up in elegant Latin, and every claim strongly urged therein against the Bishop's course. The petition was handed to the Bishop, who gave it careful consideration, endorsing it in such a manner that it could be presented to Mgr. Satolli, without prejudice to the petitioners. The occasion of the Apostolic Delegate's visit to the Josephinum of this city, in the latter part of June, was taken advantage of, and a representative committee awaited upon His Excellency, and presented the petition to him.

Early and earnest consideration was promised to the matter, and scarcely a week elapsed ere the response was received. It is still stronger than the former reply, and strengthens thereby the Bishop's position.

The following is the letter of the Apostolic Delegate : —

WASHINGTON, D. C., *July* 3, 1894.

To MR. THEODORE J. ZWESCHPER.

Dear Sir :—I answer your letter, which together with the document inclosed therein (The Bishop's letter), you handed me during my stay in Columbus.

Of course, you are aware that, as it belongs to the office of a Bishop to observe in his own diocese what is hurtful or helpful to the spiritual good of the faithful, so it belongs to his power to command, prohibit, counsel or permit whatever he judges to contribute to the discharge of his own duty, and to the good of the faithful.

The decree of the Rt. Rev. Bishop of Columbus, concerning Catholic societies and the abstaining from intoxicating liquors, ought by no means be subject to the judgment of every private individual, or of every association of simple Catholics or citizens; but every conscientious Catholic must hold for certain that the Bishop has commanded those things which seem to be for the greater good of the faithful, and the honor of every Catholic society.

Those three points, which are expressed in the letter of the Rt. Rev. Bishop, have the approval not only of Catholics, but of non-Catholics of your city; because they are not only in harmony with the laws of the Church, but they are also seasonable and necessary for the honor of the Church, especially in the State of Ohio.

Therefore, those things which the Right Rev. Bishop has commanded in his decree I approve and I decide that they are to be observed.

But, if perhaps they for the time being, seem to hurt the business of some, it will have to be patiently borne for the good of the many, and for the honor of our Holy Catholic Church.

Be of good heart, and obey faithfully what the Right Rev. Bishop has decreed, confident that Divine Providence rewards the spirit of obedience not only in the future, but also in the present life.

Faithfully in Dno,

FRANCIS, ARCHBISHOP SATOLLI,
Apostolic Delegate.

TO THE BUFFALO C. T. A. UNION.

WASHINGTON, D. C., *September* 12th, 1894.

MESSRS. G. ZWYSCHER, J. E. TRAVERS, A. McLEAN, *committee of the Buffalo Catholic Temperance Union.*

Gentlemen:—It is a pleasure for me to express to you, and through you, to those whom you represent, the satisfaction I feel in receiving the letter you kindly sent me.

The aim and work of your Union, are highly commendable.

It should be encouraged and fostered by every reflecting and upright man, who has at heart, not merely the glory of the Catholic religion, but also the welfare of his country.

Who can deny that the abuse of intoxicating drinks is a great evil, and that its consequences are deplorable? It would seem that drunkenness was quite prevalent at the first preaching of the

123

gospel; and probably even among the Jews, for
they had already degenerated from the piety of
their fathers.

Hence, St. Paul, in his epistles, declares that
drunkards, like other evil-doers, are excluded
from the Kingdom of Christ.

It would take too long to give here, the
legislation and the discipline of the Church
on this head.

Now, we must always, especially in the matter
of eating and drinking, distinguish between the
use and abuse, between moderation and excess.

But, as in the Catholic Church, counsels are
distinguished from precepts, and as the object of
the evangelical counsels is to insure the observance of the precepts, so likewise, the purpose of
total abstinence in the Catholic Church is to
withhold her children from the abuse of intoxicating drinks. It frequently happens that *total*
abstinence, is the sole sure remedy for this
abuse, particularly in the exciting business life,
and sparkling, brilliant atmosphere of ardent
America. It restores and preserves that temperance, which constitutes the physical and moral
strength of body and soul alike. Total abstinence

is a safeguard of the individual, of the family, and of society.

Thanking you, for your kind sentiments, etc.

FRANCIS, ARCHBISHOP SATOLLI,
Apostolic Delegate.

PART V.

Speech at St. Paul.

THE ADDRESS AT ST. PAUL, MINN.

In the summer of 1893, Mgr. Satolli, attended by a number of clerics, among whom were several professors of the Catholic University at Washington, D. C., made an extended tour to the Pacific.

In the course of his journey he made several speeches. The most notable was delivered at Seattle, Wash. We here give it:

As I came to this pleasant city it came to my mind that it, in its position and surroundings, is one of the most noble in the ranks of the great cities of the United States. Its scenery and situation are fully the equal of any in the world, and with all its surrounding wealth it should become to the West what New York is to the East. In traveling through the West, the remarkable enterprise, the push of the people, is what impressed me most. With this enterprise and her natural advantages, Seattle should become one of the emporiums and great seaports of the world. The scenery so grand, with moun-

9   129

tains surrounding and a wealth of fertile soil, backed with enterprise of people, who are not only active, but wonderfully intelligent, suggest the hope that here will arise one of the great cities of the world. To material welfare and enterprise, however, must be added morality. Wealth can produce no lasting welfare, unless based on moral life. Christianity is that which makes both go hand in hand. Pope Leo has at heart the prosperity and progress of the human race, and he has repeatedly tried to show the world in his various encyclicals, that material prosperity, in all lands and climes and under all forms of government, must go hand in hand with moral liberty. He wants to impress upon this magnificent country, where material prosperity has been so prominently developed, the duty of morality. While traveling through the West, in every new town, I noticed two buildings looming up, which, I think, are the best indices of the American character—the church and the school-house. So long as these institutions develop with your growth, confidence in the future is certain to spring from these two sources. So long as education and religion are welded together, the United States will prove an object lesson to the world, and she must prosper. It will also become the theatre where the vexed questions which now agitate the world will be solved, and it will become the teacher and savior of mankind.

On reaching St. Paul, on his return, on July 28th, His Excellency was tendered a public reception, to which, he replied as follows :- -

Citizens of St. Paul:—As from the city of Rome in the days of her world-wide supremacy radiated the highways that led to the frontier of civilization, so also from the city of St. Paul stretch iron roads following the setting sun until they are stayed by the waters of the Pacific. My journey to the further West took start from the central part of the United States, and the regal generosity of the presidents of your roads sped me hence to the western rim of the continent, and hither back again across the vast plains and mighty mountains.

Homer's hero, when he had seen with his eyes the "usages and cities of men," knew the world better than when he had read of them. My office demands that I should know the condition of the churches in the United States. Comparison of the West, with what I had seen in the East, would enable me to form a better judgment of the whole country. Moreover, it was my ardent desire to visit the bishops in the newly settled dioceses of the West; to converse with them, and to gather advice and experience from them, as I had done in the older and more flourishing dioceses of the East.

To my long and important journey, this evening's reception is a fit ending, a crowning of which I am justly proud. Ten months ago, when I landed on these shores, I was the bearer of two letters from his eminence, Cardinal Rampolla, secretary of state to our Holy Father, Leo XIII. One letter was addressed to the primate of the church in the United States, Cardinal Gibbons, introducing me to him, and through him to the Catholics of the country, as papal legate. The other recommended me to the archbishop of St. Paul. In consequence, after my first visit to the cardinal-archbishop of Baltimore, my second visit was paid last fall to the most reverend archbishop of St. Paul, on which occasion, as you say in your

address, I had the honor of meeting the ecclesiastical body of this province. That visit was
official, in compliance with the letter of introduc-
tion. This visit is one of choice and affection,
enhanced by the pleasure of this reception from
the capital city of the State of Minnesota. It
gives me reason to say to you what I heard from
the lips of the Holy Father himself, viz: That,
while holding in veneration and love, all the prelates of the American church, yet he had a special
esteem and affection for your archbishop, whose
personal fame has made the city's name like unto
itself—world-wide. The Holy Father sees in the
administration of this archdiocese, many and
great things that give him pleasure, none that
excite his displeasure, or call for the least repre-
hension. He is well aware that your archbishop
understands, and has at heart the progress of the
church in the American republic, and, that he
promotes that progress with zeal, rectitude and
prudence. The progress of the church has not
always been without difficulty. It is natural that
it should be so, considering the human element
in which that divine institution lives, the variety
of ages and races through which she has to pass.

When the external conditions, when the environment of the church, seem to demand new adaptations, it is no wonder that differences of opinion should exist for a time. Such differences cannot impair the essential life and vigor of the church, much as they seem to disturb harmony of thought and interrupt continuity of action. They set against those who hold to a past which they think should not change, those who honestly think that the signs of the present and of the future demand new readjustments if the church is to continue in harmony with the advancing race. Such differences, when the watchman on the tower of Sion has spoken, settle themselves into harmony once more, and the result of the passing disturbance has been a benefit to the church and society, and an advance both forward and upward.

You are kind enough to say that I have won the sympathy of America, and that the force of my position is in the public opinion of the United States, and the policy of Leo XIII. My mission, you say, has been in accord with the spirit and institutions of your country. Allow me to put it otherwise: Your institutions are in accord with the essential spirit of the church and her constitution. In pursuing my mission I find that I am acting out the very essence of your social and political life, and that I can be a good American because I am a good Catholic. Hence, I conclude that the church and the republic are made for each other, and should walk hand in hand, each in her own path, assuring as they go the spiritual and temporal welfare of the individual and of the community.

If you but consider on the one hand, the nature of human society, and on the other, the purpose of the Christian religion ; on the one hand, the spirit of civil liberty, on the other, the interior and exterior spirit of the church, you will see that the two should not be at war, else God's designs are violated and the good of humanity destroyed, which, over and above mere temporal existence, demands the higher boon of religion and morality. Your republic makes no laws concerning the establishment or hindrance of any religious body. It is well. But surely the meaning of this clause in your constitution is not to reject religion. For all Americans know that in morality and religion rest the chiefest main-

stay and shield of civil liberty: that your
constitution, as is well said in your address, rests
on the supremacy of law, and the supremacy of
law on the enlightened conscience of the citizen.

A disinterested study of religion, as embodied
in the Catholic church, will show that nowhere
is there a power appealing to conscience more
able to hold up your constitution above the storms
of human passions, more congenial to the spirit
of your republic, more conducive to its stability,
than the church of which you and I are children.
Time will show very soon, I trust, that as the
Church, from the enjoyment of the liberties guaranteed to her in this land, shall make progress
such as she has not known in other times and
other lands: so also shall the republic receive
from the church a corresponding benefit—the
absorption and assimilation into one common
citizenship, into the common mold of American
democracy, of all the nationalities and races
which in this land, acknowledge her sway and
influence. And this mutual benefiting shall be
clear evidence to all, and in our own days, that
security for the commonwealth lies in friendly
contact with the church.

Finally, your address alludes to the policy of Leo XIII, as being the inspiration and chief support of my own mission among you. Well, the august occupant of the Vatican glories in being known, and history will praise him, as the pacificator, the conciliator in these troublous years, ending the nineteenth century. To pacify by conciliating each nation, its laws, customs, literature, without detriment to the fundamental doctrines and discipline of the Christian faith, is the work to which his life has been devoted, and which his old age is carrying out to a certain and lasting triumph. I have no other ambition than to follow in the footsteps of him who has sent me to establish peace and harmony through conciliation, under the over-ruling supremacy of law.

I am happy to know that I have the sympathy and concurrence of this great archdiocese of St. Paul. It is expressions of good will, such as yours, that are, after the approval of the sovereign pontiff, my greatest consolation and mainstay. Citizens of St. Paul, I thank you. May the future of your city and of the Western empire whose commerce it commands be as prosperous and brilliant as your hearts can desire. And let

me assure you that you share with your archbishop the special affection and benediction of
our Holy Father, now gloriously reigning, Leo
XIII, whom heaven spare us long.

PART VI.

To Congresses.

ADDRESS AT CHICAGO.

THE DELEGATE AT THE CATHOLIC CONGRESS.

Announcement that the Delegate would be present at the session of the Catholic Columbian Congress, on the morning of the fifth of September, 1893, aroused enthusiasm to the highest pitch reached during its sittings.

The hall was thronged to its utmost capacity, when the chairman called the assembly to order. Prelates, priests, brothers, members of congregations enjoying dispensations to attend the Columbian exhibition for study, ladies and gentlemen, were in anxious expectancy of the guest whose presence was to be the most brilliant incident of an event in itself memorable.

At length the distinguished party arrived, its entrance being far more dramatic, than any designer could have planned ; the zest of the moment enhanced by the manifest unconsciousness of those who were its chief figures.

Breaking out of wild cheers near the entrance to the audience chamber, rapturous clapping of hands, impetuous waving of handkerchiefs, a wave of applause breaking out over the entire assembly, all the audience on their feet, and all

141

eyes concentrated upon the doors, and in another instant, the stalwart figure of the Archbishop of St. Paul appeared.

His radiant face aglow, his step the long alert stride so familiar wherever the heroic form is known; and with him a man whose visage, widely different, but not less characteristic, was already equally known to the assembly from its frequent reproduction.

The Delegate seemed himself as much astounded, as the still fervent assembly was charmed. His flashing black eyes shone with extraordinary emotion. He stood beside Archbishop Ireland, enthralled by the wonderful welcome that in its sincerity was matched only by its length and its ardor.

The people continued to cheer, volley after volley, reaching the great avenue upon which the congress building stood; the throngs in the thoroughfares were stopped by its echoes to ask the cause of so prolonged a demonstration of cordiality and delight.

The Delegate, travel-stained, having ridden all night to keep his appointment, and not having had even a moment for repose after reaching the city, at last secured silence, and in Italian, addressed the calmed meeting, subsiding like a tumultuous sea.

There were men and women in the audience who had heard many, perhaps most of the impassioned speakers of the day. They had never before seen or heard such speaking as Archbishop Satolli's. A considerable proportion of the audience, for it contained representatives of almost every nation of the earth, understood his fiery sentences emitted in great rapidity; but even to those not acquainted with Italian, the discourse was, to some extent, carried home by the marvelous vividness of the delivery, the warmth of the voice, the passion of the eye, the graphic and graceful gesture.

Every period was accentuated with applause, and at the close of each, cheers broke out anew.

When, with a superb salutation to the Constitution of the United States, the address ended, the scene witnessed upon the arrival of the Delegate and his escort was renewed.

Archbishop Satolli, pale with his arduous essay, and visibly touched to the soul by the manifest intelligence with which his words had been appreciated, stood bowing his acknowledgments for several moments before the audience would permit him to take his seat.

The address was then interpreted extempore, by Archbishop Ireland, as follows:—

I beg leave to repeat, in unmusical tones, a few of the thoughts that his Excellency, the most reverend Apostolic Delegate has presented to you in his own beautiful and musical Italian language. The delegate expresses his great delight to be this morning in the presence of the Catholic Columbian congress. He begs leave to offer you the salutation of the great pontiff, Leo XIII. In the name of Leo he salutes the spiritual children of the church on this American continent; in the name of Leo he salutes the great American republic herself.

It is. he says, a magnificent spectacle to see laymen, priests and bishops assembled here together to discuss the vital social problems which the modern conditions of humanity bring up before us. The advocates of error have their congresses, why should not the friends and advocates of truth have their congresses? This congress assembled here to-day will, no doubt, be productive of rich and magnificent results. You have met to show that the church, while opening to men the treasures of heaven, offers also felicity on earth. As St. Paul has said. "she is made for earth and heaven: she is the promise of the future life, and the life that is." All congresses are, so to speak, concentrations of great forces. Your object is to consider the social forces that God has provided, and to apply. as far as you can. to the special circumstances of your own time and country these great principles.

The great social forces are thought, will and action. In congress you bring before you these three great forces. Thought finds its food in truth; so in all that you do, in all the practical conclusions that you formulate you must bear in mind that they must all rest upon the eternal principles of truth. Will is the rectitude of the human heart, and until the human heart is voluntarily subjected to truth and virtue, all social reforms are impossible. Then comes action, which aims at the acquisition of the good needed for the satisfaction of mankind; and this again must be regulated by truth in thought, and by virtue in the human will. The well-being of society consists in the perfect order of the different elements toward the great scope of society. Order is the system of the different relations of the different elements, one to the other, and these relations to which men are subject are summarized in three words—God, man and nature.

Man has first of all his great duties to God, which must never be forgotten. He then has his duties to himself and to his fellow-men; and, finally, he has relations with the great world of nature, over which his action is exercised. From the several considerations of these different relations spring up the great problems, which at all times have vexed man's mind—the great problems which to-day are before us in view of the different evolutions, social and otherwise, which mark our modern needs. Your social congress

10

has convened to-day. Bear in mind that there was a first great social congress, which is to be the model of yours, which gave out the principles which must underlie your deliberations. The great social congress, the ideal and model of all others, was held when Christ, surrounded by the thousands of the children of Israel, delivered his great discourse on the mountain.

There the solution was given to human problems; there were laid down the vital principles. "Seek first the kingdom of God and its justice, and all other things shall be added unto you," says the good Book. "Seek first the kingdom of God." Look up the Divinity, whence came down all that without which man is absolutely at sea. Fill out first your duties to God, without the observance of which other duties are but a name. Seek God's justice in your relations, one with another. Be guided by the eternal law of the Most High, and then all things shall be added unto you. Know God's truth and live by God's justice, and the peace and felicity of earth shall be yours. The same great voice said, "Blessed are the poor in spirit; blessed are they who thirst after justice; blessed are the merciful."

Men should not devote their whole being and all their energies to the seeking out of mere matter. "Blessed are the poor in spirit"—that is, free and independent of the shackles of mere matter. "Blessed are they who hunger and thirst after justice"—justice first, before self-satisfaction, before all attention to one's personal wants. And "blessed are the merciful." Blessed are they who know and feel that they do not live for themselves, whose hearts go out in sweetest mercy to all their fellows. History has proven that human reason alone does not solve the great social problems. These problems were spoken of in prechristian times. Both Aristotle and Plato discussed them. But prechristian times gave us a world of slavery, when the multitude lived only for the benefit of the few.

There is evidence throughout the story of man of a divine providential design. Blind is he who sees it not, and he who studies it not courts disaster. It was when Christ brought down upon earth the great truths from the bosom of His Father, that humanity was lifted up and entered upon a new road to happiness and felicity. Christ brought to nature the additional gift of

the supernatural. Both are needed and he who
would have one without the other fails. The
supernatural comes not to destroy or eliminate
the natural, but to purify it, to elevate it, to
build it up, and hence, since the coming of
Christ, science, art, philosophy, social economy,
all studies partake of the natural as well as the
supernatural—the natural coming from man's
own thoughts and man's own actions, and the
supernatural pouring down upon those thoughts
and actions, direction, richness and grace.

To-day it is the duty of Catholics to bring into
the world the fulness of supernatural truth
and supernatural life. This is especially the
duty of a Catholic congress. There are nations
which are never separated from the church, but
which have neglected often to apply in full degree the lessons of the gospel. There are nations
that have gone out from the church, bringing
with them, many of her treasures, and because
of what they have brought, yet show virgin light;
but, cut off from the source, unless that source is
brought into close contact with them, there is
danger for them. Bring them in contact with
those divine forces by your action and your

teachings. Bring your fellow countrymen back ;
bring your country into immediate connection
with the great source of truth and light, and the
blessed influence of Christ and Christ's church.
And, in this manner shall it come to pass that
the words of the psalmist shall be fulfilled.
"Mercy and justice have you one with another :
justice and peace prevail."

Let us restore among men, justice and charity.
Let us teach men to be prompt, ever to make
sacrifice of self for the common good. This is
the foundation of all social elevating movements;
it is the foundation of your own congress. Now,
all these great principles have been marked out
in most luminous lines in the encyclicals of the
great pontiff, Leo XIII. We then study those
encyclicals : hold fast to them as the safest anchor-
age. The social questions are being studied the
world over. It is well they should be studied in
America, for here we have more than elsewhere
the keys to the future. Here in America, you
have a country blessed specially by providence in
the fertility of its fields and the liberty of its
institutions. Here you have a country which
will pay back all efforts, not merely tenfold, but

a hundredfold; and this no one understands better than the immortal Leo, and he charges his Delegate to speak out to America words of hope and blessing.

Then in conclusion, the Delegate begs of you American Catholics to be fully loyal to your great mission and to the duties which your circumstances impose upon you. Here are golden words spoken by the Delegate in concluding his discourse: "Go forward, in one hand bearing the book of christian truth and in the other the constitution of the United States." Christian truth and American liberty will make you free, happy and prosperous. They will put you on the road to progress. May your steps ever persevere on that road. Again he salutes you with all his heart. Again he expresses his delight to be with you, and again speaks forth to you in strongest and sweetest tones, the love of your Holy Father, Leo XIII.

LETTER TO THE COLORED CATHOLIC CONGRESS.

The following letter from the Apostolic Delegate, was read at the recent session of the Colored Catholic Congress in Baltimore:—

WASHINGTON, D. C., *October 6th*, 1894.

MR. WILLIAM S. LOFTON:—

Dear Sir:—I beg to answer your favor of the twentieth of September last, in which you kindly invite me to participate in the proceedings of your Congress, for which I sincerely thank you.

From the beginning of my residence in America, I have often shown my sympathy for the Colored race. Because of the religious and moral needs of this numerous family in the United States, I have been attracted to them by a sentiment of Christian charity, and I have never ceased to desire that not only Catholics, but all honest men should co-operate to improve their condition.

151

I cannot dissemble my conviction, that if the civilizing influence of Catholics had been exercised more wisely and zealously upon the Colored race, since the happy day of their liberation from the yoke of slavery, their condition would be better to-day than it is.

I have heard that there are about eight millions of Colored people in the United States : but I fear that the number of those who had attained such a degree of civilization as is becoming for American citizenship is not, comparatively speaking, very large.

I have been told that the instruction and moral education of many of them—not around here, but further South—is far from being all that could be desired.

I am pleased to know that the United States government, ever since the emancipation, has labored to free the Colored race from that moral servitude which, even in a state of freedom, is more opposed to human dignity than slavery itself.

Any institution tending to give instruction and moral education to the masses co-operates with the government in the great work of civilization.

I mean that instruction and moral education, which teaches every one his relation to God, to his family, and to society, and which teaches man the practice of his duties and rights, in order that he may attain temporal welfare in this life, and above all. the high end to which Providence has destined him.

Every one unless he is an atheist, must admit that God, the Creator of all things, has a care for all things in proportion to their very essence and nature, and therefore, he exercises a special providence over mankind, over every nation, over every family, and over every individual.

It is certain that in God's governance of the human race, very much is done through Christianity, of which the various denominations existing in this country. are expressions intrinsically and extrinsically more or less deficient, but of which the Catholic Church is the only complete and perfect expression.

It is enough to read the history of the past to recognize what has been the thought and action of the Catholic Church in regard to the slave trade.

Among the very numerous bands of Catholic heroes, who have consecrated their lives to the welfare of the Colored race, stands preëminent, Saint Peter Claver, after whom you have very properly named your Union. The future history of the civilization of the Colored people will require many a page to relate how Leo XIII has ever had at heart the abolition of the slave trade in Africa, and to tell what he has done to further the civilization of the Colored race.

From this we conclude, that the co-operation that the Catholic church, with the United States government, lends to the action of the government for the civilization of the Colored people, must largely contribute to the ultimate success of such efforts.

I do not intend here, to discuss the question of how much good has been done to the Colored race by the Protestant sects; nor what advantages the same race have derived from the civilizing action of Protestants, but, I do maintain that the action of the Catholic Church will be productive of still greater results. This is patent to all who will look into the matter. It is evidenced by what she accomplishes within her own body, and what she induces others to do by her influence, whether exercised directly or indirectly.

I have already mentioned the usefulness of that instruction and moral education, which are calculated by their very nature to lead men to the practice of their obligations and rights; but here the greatest care should be taken to follow the proper method and to avoid extremes.

To talk to a man of nothing but his obligations, and to exaggerate and continually harp on his duties, does not elevate his character, but tends to render it servile.

For a man to talk exclusively of his rights and to insist upon his claims on others, tends to license.

The one way of acting degrades and dejects; the other exalts and turns the head. There is still a third method of civilizing, according to which a man should know and demand his rights before learning and practising his duties; but it is certain that, although in some particular cases right may precede duty still, absolutely speaking, duty precedes right, just as cause precedes effect, and just as the end precedes the means taken to reach that end.

I am of the opinion, that the true and proper way to civilize both the individual and the mass of society, is that which teaches a man at one and the same time, his rights and his obligations, and which leads him both to assert his rights and to fulfil his duties towards others.

This is the fundamental principle of the science of Catholic pedagogics, or I might say, the principle of Divine pedagogy for the human race, from the creation, to the coming of Christ; and this is the teaching principle which, from the coming of Christ, to the present day, has been continuously taught by the Catholic Church.

St. Paul gives this general rule of pedagogy in these words:

"For the grace of God our Saviour hath appeared to all men, instructing us that, denying ungodliness and worldly desires, we should live soberly and justly, and godly in this world, looking for the blessed hope and coming of the glory of the Great God and our Saviour Jesus Christ."—Tit., Chap. II, vv. 11–13.

We should especially mark these words:— "God our Saviour" and "to all men." For Who or What is it that teaches us of "God our Saviour?" and Who or What is it that hath appeared "to all men?"

Hence we must conclude, that without the *grace of God our Saviour*, no civilization is possible; and *all men*, without exception, are required to listen with docility to the instructions which He pleases to give them.

As the sculptor first removes the obstacle to the work by chipping off the useless portions of the marble before giving the statue the form intended, so, too, the first thing to be done in civilizing and Christianizing any man is to remove the obstacles thereto, which consist in the contrary dispositions of the human heart; and these unfavorable dispositions are, according to St. Paul, *ungodliness and worldly desires;* but it is necessary, not only to avoid vice, but to practise virtue;

(*a*) towards one's self, by sobriety and moderation;

(*b*) towards the family and society, by the practice of justice;

(*c*) towards God, by the practice of religious duties.

"We should live soberly, and justly, and godly in this world." As every art has its proximate and final end, so, according to St. Paul, civilization is of such a nature, as to tend to secure a man's temporal welfare in this world, and through religion, to ensure his eternal happiness in the world to come. Every man should aspire and strive to attain this end, with all the ardor of his soul, hoping to reap it through the grace of God, our Saviour, looking for the blessed hope and coming of the glory of the Great God, and our Saviour, Jesus Christ.

Besides the Catholic institutions of various kinds already established for the purpose of promoting the welfare, civil, moral and religious, of the Colored race, congresses of laymen aiming at concerted action for these noble purposes, must be of great value.

I therefore congratulate you, on your courage in undertaking this congress, hoping that it may result in wise and practical resolutions, for the improvement of your race, and that the success of this congress may lead to others, in order to attain always, more and more efficaciously, the end described in this letter.

Blessing you and your convention, I remain,

Yours in Xto.,

FRANCIS, ARCHBISHOP SATOLLI,
Delegate Apostolic.

PART VII.

The Press.

THE FOURTH POWER.

THE PLACE OF THE PRESS IN THE PUBLIC LIFE.

At the annual banquet of the Gridiron Club, on January 26th, 1895, at Washington, D. C., the following plea for the Press came from Mgr. Satolli, in whose name his secretary, V. Rev. Dr. Rooker, spoke. The address is:—

From Aristotle to the renowned author of "L'Esprit des Lois" learned men have divided the functions of government into classes, the legislative, the executive or administrative, and the judicial, which are, in truth, but three activities of one and the same power, which is vested in him who has the care of the people and represents them. Now, however, an adequate division of the powers of government would have to include a fourth element, and this is public opinion, exercising its activity through the organism of the public press. It is consequently a great

11   **161**

pleasure and honor to me to be with you this
evening, feeling, as I do, that I am surrounded
by the representatives of this fourth power in the
greatest and most glorious of modern republics—
a republic emulous of the glory of those of ancient
times. A half century ago one of the principal
periodicals of Europe, the *Civilta Cattolica*, at the
beginning of its existence, said: "It happens
naturally that in those countries where journalism is in vogue it comes to be a true, perhaps
even the supreme social power, it being received
as an axiom that the public opinion is the mistress
and queen of the world. This public opinion
has no other means of making itself felt, nor
organ for its manifestation, more efficacious than
journalism."

And Bryce, in his admirable work on the
"American Commonwealth," declares: "In no
country is public opinion so powerful as in the
United States; in no country can it be so well
studied; yet opinion has really been the chief and
ultimate power in nearly all nations at nearly all
times. I mean the opinion, unspoken, uncon-
scious, but not the less real and potent, of the
masses of the people." And it is the public press

which has the most real and efficacious influence in constituting, moderating, keeping alive and modifying when necessity requires public opinion. It is a question whether laws depend from the social dispositions of the people or whether the social dispositions depend from the laws. In my opinion the dependence is mutual, and consequently the legislative power cannot hold itself independent of nor indifferent to the popular opinion which manifests itself through the press.

Man, as a social being, has three natural needs—the communication of his ideas, interest and participation in the government of the State to which he belongs, to be kept as accurately and promptly as possible informed of what goes on in the world about him. Nothing better meets these three wants than the press. If men were left with the faculty of speech alone, none of these three needs would be satisfied. Books are, it is true, a useful expedient, but rather serve for general instruction than for the practical knowledge of the daily course of events, and may be fittingly called the "fixed press." Periodicals answer the need better, but not sufficiently, as experience proves they

may be termed an "intermittent press." The
daily or public press, a continuous press, when
well organized, has the advantage of being fully
proportionate to the social exigencies of the
human mind. The practical life, not only of the
individual, but also of the body politic, is a
syllogism, the major proposition of which con-
taining a general truth may be found in the book
press, the minor may be had from the periodicals,
but to draw the conclusion belongs properly to
the daily public press, which, day by day describes the social life in its minutest details.
And, therefore, just as the conclusion of the
syllogism contains in itself all the strength of
the premises and is distinct from them, so the
public press contains all the force of general
truths and of particular applications, describing
as in its proper field that which is done in practical life as well by the governing, as by the
governed.

Society is an organized body. The government is its head, the people its members, the
military its nerves and muscles, its blood the
wealth which has its beginning and end in the
industry of the people; morality and religion

are its heart, the press may well be called its lungs, since it serves as the organ of public respiration. Or, again, I do not hesitate to say that in the body politic, the public press has that office which in the individual, is performed by conscience, and to define it as the organ of social conscience. In fact, what are the functions of conscience? To testify, to withhold and instigate, to accuse, to reprehend and to cause remorse. All these things follow the application of what we know to what we do, and this application is threefold: First, when we recognize that we have, or have not done something, and in this way conscience is said to testify; next, when we judge that we ought or ought not to do something, and so conscience instigates or withholds, and finally, when we judge that what we have done was well or badly done, and then conscience accuses, approves or reprehends. And is it not the public press which makes known the deeds of society, from day to day? Charles Dudley Warner declares that the purpose of the creation of the newspaper is that it should be a "mirror of contemporary life." Is it not the public press which, at the proper time, should make known to the makers of law, what should, or should not be done for the common welfare? Can any one deny to the public press the right, in matters which concern the people at large, to estimate the value of public acts? And especially does the public press act as the public conscience, since the mass of the people think, speak and act under the influence of impressions received from their daily papers.

Up to the fifteenth century there was no vehicle of intellectual and moral light, except the manuscript codices for the few and monuments and the spoken word for the many; and, therefore, it was more necessary than in our time to have monuments, pictures and statues, by the sight of which the youth might be inspired to imitate the generous and the glorious acts of heroic men. The Hebrews at the time of their greatest glory had their temples and tombs. The Greeks had their temples, statues and pictures. The Romans had their trophies, columns and arches, and to-day, even in her treasures of monumental literature, can be read without books the record of centuries of civil, religious and moral virtues. Then followed the days of schools and universities, which became the centres and sources of knowledge. From the invention of printing in the fifteenth century to the eighteenth, books were multiplied and instruction facilitated and generalized, and libraries sprang up like so many temples of the human encyclopædia. It was left for the public press to provide fully and universally for the teaching of the masses. So great being the importance of the public press, it is evident how much those who labor in this ministry merit the good will and esteem of the people.

I cannot agree with Mr. J. W. Keller, who makes of journalism a mere trade, and a poor one at that. To me it seems a life of devotion to high and noble work, to the enlightenment and betterment of mankind, and brings with it that reward, richer than the mere accumulation of wealth, the consciousness of being a factor in the onward progress of humanity. If, then, the public press is a kind of social priesthood, one can easily understand that those who administer it should be conscious of their high office, and conform always to the rules of sacred duty. I may not be indiscreet in suggesting that over the door of every newspaper building should be inscribed the words, "Truth, Justice, Honesty. Of All, for All."

From the day of my arrival in America down to the present moment, I have had every reason to feel with the press of this country; to conceive the most exalted opinion of it; to appreciate its great importance; to nourish for it feelings of sincere and imperishable gratitude. If you desire to know my mission among you, you will find it expressed in the conditions enunciated for my favorable reception here by a well-meaning but misled writer in the *Forum*, two years ago. It is to help "to teach the ignorant, to raise the fallen, to lead the guilty and penitent to the invisible and Divine Saviour, who alone has power to forgive sin, to console the sorrowing, to edify the believing, to promote righteousness, liberty, sympathy and the spirit of Christian brotherhood throughout the land."

If you want to know what my mission is not you have it in the words of this same writer, in which he explains what he thinks it is. He asserts that I am here to further the claims of the Pope to "a kingdom of this world," "a kingdom which embraces the whole world," "all the kingdoms of the world and the glory of them." In my own name and in that of Leo XIII, who sent me, I repudiate any such purpose. And when it shall please the Pope to recall me, trusting in the kindness and recti-tude of the public press, as Samuel of old on laying down the government of Israel appealed to the assembled people to express their satis-faction or dissatisfaction with his administration, so I shall not hesitate to present to the press of the country, the record of my labors, and say, " Judge me."

PART VIII.

Jubilees and Dedications.

CENTENARY OF THE CATHOLIC HIERARCHY.

HELD IN BALTIMORE, NOVEMBER 10TH, 1889.

The following speech is mentioned by His Eminence, Cardinal Gibbons, in his preface.

It is regrettable that no extended report of this felicitous after-dinner speech is in existence, for we are assured that it was most enjoyable.

This was the first public speech made by the Archbishop of Lepanto on American soil. During its delivery, he was repeatedly applauded; his reference to the Pope's friendship for America aroused a storm of applause, while the hope held out in the conclusion, that some future Pope would visit the United States, coming from such a source, is calculated to make every American Christian's heart throb with joy, at the thought of seeing on American soil the successor of St. Peter, the Apostle.

When the dinner was over, His Eminence, Cardinal Gibbons, arose and stated that a cablegram had been received from the Pope in reference to the Centennial.

At his request, the message was read by Very Rev. Dr. O'Connell, Rector of the American College at Rome. It was dated at Rome, November 9th, and was addressed to the Most Eminent Cardinal Gibbons, Archbishop of Baltimore, U. S. A. The wording was in Latin, as follows:—

"Solemnitas qua saecularis erectionis episcopatus Americani memoria celebrata est magnae nobis jucunditati fuit. Dum fausta quaeque Americanae ecclesiae ominamur petitam benedictionem peramanter impertimur.

LEO XIII, P. P."

The following is a free translation of the message:—

The solemn celebration of the one hundredth anniversary of the establishment of the American Hierarchy, has given us cause for great joy. While we wish every prosperity for the American Church, we most cheerfully grant it our Apostolic Benediction.

After the cablegram had been read, Cardinal Gibbons proposed the health of the Pope, and Archbishop Satolli, as the representative of the Holy See, responded:—

I should speak in English, but I am not sufficiently well acquainted with that language. There are no reasons wanting why the Latin tongue, in which I will speak, is not more appropriate on the present occasion.

First, because it is universal, and secondly, because it is the language of the ancient Rome, whose institutions American people have not only imitated, but even emulated.

In the very solemn celebration in the church to-day, it seemed to me even as though I were in Rome, because of my surroundings.

The only thing wanting, was the presence of the Supreme Pontiff, but, I can assure you of his presence here in spirit.

The present Pontiff, at the moment of his election, turned his thoughts to the great American nation, and he was greatly pleased by its religious progress. He saw that the special designs of Providence, hung over this nation, and he was fully persuaded of the great progress which Catholicity would make, even under his own Pontificate.

This Church, therefore, became the subject of his especial predilection and solicitude, and he seized every occasion to display his love and especial affection for it.

Of this, the Bishops and all other Catholics

who have ever visited Rome, have had evident proofs. The Holy Father aimed at having the great national council held at Baltimore, and under his protection and Apostolic approbation, it succeeded, not only as splendidly as the others, but even surpassed them. Another proof of his good will he gave the moment he heard of the Bishops founding the Catholic University. Not only did he encourage this, but even gave his Apostolic sanction to the constitution of the University, by a special brief.

Finally, in this very year he added proof of his care, by taking part in this Centennial Feast of the Catholic Hierarchy, by sending a Papal representative.

Although, the Holy Father finds himself at the present time, borne down by bitter tribulations, he none the less experiences great relief and rejoicing of heart when he turns to the Church in free America.

He never doubts the generosity and filial devotion of American Catholics. For he believes that the spirit of liberty which they enjoy in their own country, makes them desirous that the Sovereign Pontiff should regain that independence and liberty which appertain to him by Divine institution, as the head of the Universal Church, and as the representative of the person and authority of Christ.

Under more favorable circumstances, Leo XIII, or his successor, whoever he may be, will some day find pleasure in visiting in person, this great American nation.

Then, indeed, will your hearts be glad and rejoice, strong in presence of the Holy Father among you, and he will bedew and refresh you and your nation with new benedictions.

———

SILVER EPISCOPAL JUBILEE OF RT. REV. BISHOP S. V. RYAN.

On the 8th of November, 1893, the much loved and venerable Bishop Ryan of Buffalo, celebrated the silver jubilee of his episcopal ordination. A large gathering of distinguished prelates, clergymen and laity were present.

The Delegate spoke as follows:—

It is a sincere pleasure to me to gratify a long-entertained desire of visiting your beautiful city, which, if smaller than a few others in size and number of inhabitants, is, however, not unequal to the greatest in the pursuits of industry, the beauty of its broad streets and avenues, and in the elegance of its public and private buildings.

The energy of your enterprise, the nobility of your sentiments, the generosity of your good deeds, have not, however, been unknown to me, and to-day I see that the reality far surpasses the report which has gone abroad concerning them.

178

While both the clergy and the faithful have vied with each other in celebrating the jubilee of their Bishop, both have given solemn proof that he, in the twenty-five years of his episcopal ministry, has carried to their highest development the interests of the Catholic religion; that he has, by his good works, merited and received the esteem and affection of his fellow-citizens.

I feel assured that the name of Bishop Stephen Vincent Ryan will go down to posterity loaded with honors

In the discharge of his episcopal ministry, Bishop Ryan has confirmed that truth, ever old yet ever new, the truth that the most deserving citizens are they who strive to increase the spiritual welfare of their fellows by the preaching of Christian Truth, by the founding of institutions dedicated to the education of youth, and by establishing institutions devoted to the work of alleviating human miseries and misfortunes.

It is not enough to know, not enough to be zealous to do many and great things for the good of Christianity—nay, rather one must have rectitude of purpose, tranquil firmness of execution, and prudence of action.

It is not enough to be animated by general principles of right and justice; one must know how to apply those principles with moderation and charity.

By this, I intend to bestow on your Bishop, a well-deserved eulogy. And as he would never have been able to bring to a happy termination so many great undertakings, without the constant and generous aid of his clergy and people, so I mean also, to bestow the same richly merited praise on all here present, and through them, on all the citizens of Buffalo.

Here and there are found some obstinate adversaries of the Catholic Church who, to accomplish their purpose, use untruth and calumny, means proportionate to the end which they have in view.

These men do not understand our affairs nor our institutions, but in their prejudice, they imagine them to be what they are not. In a thousand ways they continue to combat the Church and her institutions, as though they were hostile and harmful to the political and civil institutions of the country:—in fine, they claim that they are unable to see how the spirit of

Catholicism can be in harmony with the American Constitution and with American liberties, as these were understood by their great founder, Washington.

The Constitution adopted under the guidance of Washington, prohibited any law by which the civil power might seem to enter the sphere of religion. And that great man, in whom America has her Solon and her Cincinnatus, could not have done otherwise. I believe that no man living understands better the purpose which animated Washington, than the great Pontiff Leo XIII, just as I believe no man living understands the mind of Leo, as Washington would understand it, were he alive to-day to study it.

In many ways might I show that this opposition is based on imagination, is unfounded; that it is false—even that it is harmful to the security of American liberty.

Catholics have already demonstrated clearly and gloriously, both in the administration of public affairs and under arms, that they are the staunchest upholders of the Republic in days of peace, and are her most valiant defenders in time of war.

Our Catholic institutions are adapted to alleviate every form of human ill. They are unfailing fountains of civil virtues. Furthermore, the generation which grows up imbued with the Catholic spirit by means of our churches, schools and colleges, offers great hope for the lasting prosperity of the common country.

St. Thomas, on the authority of St Augustine, says that free institutions are a precious gift of divine Providence to a virtuous people. Consequently, free institutions will last the longer, and be productive of the most beneficial results, and most effective of every civic virtue, just in proportion as a people keeps itself in conformity with the designs of Divine Providence, and in the direct path toward the destiny which Divine Providence has marked out for it.

The highest aim of the civil power is to render its subjects more and more virtuous, and, therefore. it has the corresponding duty of appreciating and aiding the institutions, which tend to make men truly virtuous, with respect to God and their fellows.

Hence, it is clearly evident that the Catholic Church is the true and earnest friend of the

American Republic. And, on the other hand, I venture to say that, whatever antagonizes the Church, or her institutions, is an attempt, more or less direct, against the liberties guaranteed by your Constitution.

In these few words I have expressed to you my conviction, touching the relation between the Catholic Church and your Constitution. I wish you every happiness, and I beg you to accept the sincere wish of my heart, that in the shortest possible time, the Church may increase the number of her faithful by millions, and that the Republic may have the good fortune and the glory to find in these increased millions, so many faithful and valiant citizens.

May such be your future.

GOLDEN JUBILEE OF REV. J. B. HESPELEIN, C. SS. R.

In the following address, Mgr. Satolli touches upon the relations between Church and State, and the subject of missions to non-Catholics.

The occasion was the golden jubilee of Rev. J. B. Hespelein, C. SS. R., celebrated at the Church of the Redemptorist Fathers, on Girard Avenue, Philadelphia, Pa., on the 10th of September, 1894.

Many interesting speeches had been made at dinner, among them one by Dr. Schroeder, of the Catholic University, Washington, D. C., when Mgr. Satolli rose to speak. He said:—

Among the many items collected from all parts of the country to fill the pages of the daily papers, there was one a few days ago, stating that a family feast would be celebrated in Philadelphia, by the Redemptorist Fathers, on the occasion of the Golden Jubilee of the Reverend Father Hespelein.

It was reported, too, that the Apostolic Delegate and the Most Rev. Archbishop of Philadelphia would be among the guests. This time the papers stated the truth, and I shall add, that it is with good reason that a golden jubilee is celebrated, since the fortune of reaching it becomes daily rarer.

To be present at this solemnity affords me much pleasure, especially since it gives me the opportunity to meet again your Most Rev. Archbishop.

Furthermore, I am much gratified on this occasion, by the thought that it is now more than fifty years since the disciples of St. Alphonsus determined to cross the Atlantic, to impart to this country the fruits of their apostleship.

If we look at the great benefits already obtained through their ministry in this country, we soon discover that the determination of coming here was praiseworthy in its aim, beneficial in its effects, and has ever been carried out in conformity with the spirit of your Congregation and of your holy founder himself.

From the results it is also easy to show that if your Congregation has its particular standard and character in exercising the holy ministry, America is the fittest field wherein to develop the work of its ministry and zeal.

Those who are familiar with the life of your holy founder, find no difficulty in believing that St. Alphonsus, who not improbably foresaw the beginning and the progress of the American Republic, would, had he continued to live, have preferred to exercise his pastoral zeal in America; and, in addition, that he would have chosen to write his works here, rather than under the government of the place in which he spent his life. I refer to that tyrant and hypocrite, Minister Tannucci, whose censures the holy doctor feared for himself and his congregation, when he published not only his Moral Theology, but even his other works of devotion.

From the works written by the holy doctor, it can be easily understood that while his theological system is comprehensive, his dogmatic and moral doctrines and even his ascetic principles, in regard to ecclesiastics and laymen, find the easiest and most efficacious application here in America.

And here be kind enough to allow me this digression.

The position of the Catholic Church may be regarded by the State, in three different points of view.

First, when the Catholic Church is considered to be an institution opposed to the State, and therefore, as such to be crushed by all means.

This was the position of the Roman Empire towards the Catholic Church, during the first three centuries of her existence, and such it would be wheresoever by any chance the system of the idolatry of humanity should happen to predominate, socially and politically.

The second point of view as to the standing of the Church, in regard to the State, is when the State recognizes the Catholic Church not only as a society, legally existent as any other religious, moral or scientific association, but also as a subsistent, divine and juridical society, belonging by her nature to a superior and universal order.

And thus she was undoubtedly regarded by the Christian state, from the epoch of Constantine until the sixteenth century.

The third point of view is when the State, as to its being and action, does not recognize the Catholic Church nor the spirit of the Christian law and doctrine, and only recognizes her as a society existing in the State, but not as a society juridically subsisting.

And this is the condition in which, owing to the work begun in the sixteenth century, and continued since by degrees, the Catholic Church is held nowadays by the modern states according to their several constitutions.

We should observe that this third status is just half way between the first and second. Consequently, touching in a measure both extremes, it is looked upon in different ways, and is thereby more or less satisfactory to the Church.

But in truth, the Catholic Church has nothing to fear, nor does she fear in any wise, from the Republic.

For the Constitution, the loyalty of the public officers to their principles, and the prudence of the citizens are all guarantees of safety.

If I am not mistaken I have here depicted the characteristic feature of the history of the Catholic Church and of mankind from Christ up to date, and perhaps till the end of the world. In other words I have indicated the criterion of the philosophy of universal history.

Before closing I would like to express an idea, which I am sure would meet the approbation of your holy founder.

My idea is that your Order send learned preachers throughout the country to the cities, to the towns, to the villages, to spread the light of Catholic truth among the masses. The end of this mission should be, that those who do not share our faith should be first disabused of all the prejudices that up the present have prevented them from entering the flock of Christ, and then, being enlightened by a simple, but clear exposition of Catholic truth, they should be attracted by its beauty, feel inclined to love it, and finally helped by divine grace, should decide to embrace it.

I have repeatedly been told, that preaching has hitherto been confined to Catholic congregations of hearers; that there is a great need of a more general and efficient action, in order to co-operate with the designs of Providence for the conversion of the non-Catholics.

No one is allowed to read the Book of Divine Predestination, but I venture to say that such is the design, not to say the law, made by our Lord, and expressed by St. Paul, in these words:—"How shall they believe in Him they have not heard, and how shall they hear with-

out a preacher, and how shall they preach
except they be sent."

But as to being sent, the mission exists, especially for your congregation.

It is sad to consider the immense losses
of the Catholic Church in this country. For
while, according to statistics, over twenty millions of Catholics have come to this country,
the members of our Church number now about
ten millions.

On the other hand, a great many of the Protestants are so well disposed towards our Church,
that we can repeat the words of Christ to the
apostles: "Behold, I say unto you, lift up your
eyes, and look on the fields that now are white
already with harvest."

Therefore, I beg to express my heartfelt wishes
that the Catholic Church may rally her children
by millions through the zealous work of the
Redemptorists, thus earning a new crown of
glory for your congregation on earth, and for your
Holy Founder in heaven.

In closing, I repeat my sincere congratulations
to the Rev. Father Hespelein;—nay, I wish all
the Redemptorists here present may celebrate

their golden jubilee, and to the Most Rev. Arch-bishop, I say, I consider myself invited to be present at the celebration of the golden jubilee, not only of his ordination, but also of his episcopal consecration.

———

At the ceremony of erecting the Stations of the Cross in St. Mary's Church, Poughkeepsie, N. Y., on March 12th, 1894, Mgr. Satolli was present by request of the Pastor, Rev. Dr. Nilan.

To meet him, had come, at the pastor's invitation, the Mayor of the City, General Smith, U. S. A., and other distinguished guests.

Mgr. Satolli, recognizing the gentlemen named as representatives of their orders, spoke on Church, State and the Army. His words were :—

I feel highly gratified and honored not only by the distinguished assemblage of so many citizens both of the clergy and of the laity, but also by the kind words addressed to me by the two gentlemen representing the civil and military power.

The wise have always believed that harmony is one of the chief factors in development. This belief is triumphantly illustrated in this country. For, whilst a long course of seven centuries was necessary for the development of the Roman

192

Republic, but a single century sufficed for the American Republic to reach the results of the present time. Results that command the admiration of the world. This is, indeed, a civil achievement to which the history of the human race will never produce a parallel.

The cause of this is to be looked for, not only in the wisdom of the founders of this Republic, but, also, in the harmony and co-operation of all for the common weal.

It is explained, moreover, by the generous sacrifices which so many have made towards the greatness of their common country, and its ever-increasing glory.

Let me utter my conviction, that as long as the American people strive to strengthen the bond of fraternal love, and as long as they generously vie with one another in advancing true progress, the American Republic will never be wanting in peace and general welfare.

But the glory of the United States should not be based solely on material prosperity. Justice, well-regulated liberty, and continued efforts towards truth and virtue, constitute the solid basis, which assures to this country a never-fading

13

glory. Three orders, the religious, the civil and the military, are the elements of national life, as was substantially taught by the great philosopher and statesmen, Aristotle. It is, therefore, a great satisfaction that persons representing these orders are here together to-day. I mean the Mayor representing civil authority, the General representing the military, and ourselves representing the religious order. Let us always remain united in this peaceful harmony. For this purpose it is necessary that any feeling of dislike, any idea of prejudice, or any cause of distrust be eliminated. No one will deny that union and co-operation are desirable and useful for the common good. For the direction of the religious ministry, we have the solicitous and wise authority of the ecclesiastical hierarchy, directed by the Pope, the supreme Pastor, who has from Christ the authority and duty of spiritual teacher and ruler. He is Catholic, that is, universal. By the nature of his office, he has no nationality; he is American, as well as Italian. And, we are glad to say, that the essential character of the Papacy shines with special splendor in the venerated person of Leo the XIII, by reason of his singular qualities, and of the policy which, during the sixteen years of his Pontificate, he has displayed in literature, and in the political, natural, and theological sciences. Let me add history to this list, for, it is well known that to its study, he has given a powerful impetus by throwing open to public use the archives of the Vatican; and finally, in the moderation and peace-loving character which has distinguished his policy. Now, in the presence of Leo XIII, there can be no shadow of foundation for the suspicion, that Papal authority, and the influence of the Catholic Church are not in perfect accord with that spirit of justice, liberty and fraternity, on which depends the welfare of a people.

The accord and relations which exist between Roman—i. e. Civil, and Canon Law, with the universal approval and consent of jurists, are a guarantee of perpetual harmony.

For such harmony must surely characterize the government of men in both civil and religious progress.

Because it is a harmony arising not from the caprice of man, but from law, ecclesiastical and civil.

To illustrate this it is a pleasure to point in a special manner to the acts of the Most Rev. Archbishop of New York, nor must we forget to pay a tribute of well-deserved praise to the pastor of this church. The former, as head of this Metropolitan Diocese, and the latter, in his pastoral office here at St. Mary's, have both shown that the spirit of the Christian Church is no wise antagonistic to the sentiments of pastoral charity, and that the endeavor to promote the progress of Christian Faith is in line with the endeavor to secure civil perfection.

We are greatly pleased to have the opportunity of greeting the Mayor, and of wishing him every happiness, recognizing and respecting, as we do, in his person the civil government.

It is proper, also, that we should show special respect, and wish health and happiness to General Smith, as the representative of that military power, which, while not rashly bent on new conquests, is ever ready to guarantee peace to the country, and to defend it bravely against hostile aggression.

I, therefore, invite you all to join with me in paying regard to and in proposing the health of the Mayor, of the General, and of all present, with the fervent wish, that, just as we are all together here at the same fraternal board, so the same principle of truth and of morality, of religion and of knowledge may bind together all Americans. And it will be easy for us reach that happy goal, if we strive to know the truth, and knowing it, we embrace it in the luminous field of doctrine, of morality, and of history.

ADDRESS AT THE SEE-HOUSE OF THE DIOCESE OF NEW YORK.

On August 15th, 1894, Mgr. Satolli sung Pontifical Mass in New York Cathedral.

The Most Rev. Archbishop Corrigan preached eloquently on filial duty to the Holy Father. He afterwards entertained at dinner Mgr. Satolli, who, in response to the usual toasts, had the Rev. Dr. Papi, Secretary of the Apostolic Delegation, read the following address :—

The Most Rev. Apostolic Delegate in the first place thanks the Most Rev. Archbishop of New York for the gracious toast offered in his honor.

It gives him great joy to be in New York on this great Feast of the Blessed Virgin Mary. It pleases him to be encircled by this chosen gathering of gentlemen, because their presence is intended not only to honor his own person, but also that of Archbishop Corrigan ; and both of them, Mgr. Satolli as Apostolic Delegate, and Mgr. Corrigan as Archbishop of New York, representing the Holy Father.

198

He is delighted on this beautiful Feast day also to send a greeting to this illustrious diocese, which for many reasons, holds one of the very first places in the Catholic Church in the United States, and which deserves all praise, because, while keeping fully abreast with the civil progress of the country, it has shown itself no less solicitous for religious than for earthly advancement.

If we need a proof of this, we need but to look around us to see her magnificent cathedral and churches, her institutions, her schools, her asylums, her hospitals, her homes for the aged and infirm; they have arisen from nothing, and are now towering aloft all over the diocese, giving ample testimony to the civilizing and refining effect of the Church on all classes of society.

There is one work, however, which is eminent above all the others, and which forms a fitting complement to the grand institutions of this diocese, and that is the noble building now approaching completion, the seminary on Valentine Hill, whose object and sole purpose is to bring every advantage to the clergy and to the people.

And if his grace, the Most Rev. Archbishop, deserves praise for accomplishing so much by his labor, by his words and by his administration, if the clergy for their zeal and co-operation merit a share in this glory, it is but just also, to acknowledge the magnificent aid given by the faithful of the diocese, who have assisted the Archbishop and the priests, and enabled them to complete so much by their sympathy, their counsel, and their willing contribution of the pecuniary resources wherewith God and their own favor have endowed them. And it is of this account that the Most Rev. Delegate, while proposing first of all the health of the Archbishop of New York, believes that he divines the wishes of the Archbishop in proposing the health also of the Reverend clergy here present, who so worthily represent the zealous ministry of the diocese: and of the distinguished laymen present here to-day, giving testimony of the faith that is living and flourishing among the good people of New York.

PART IX.

To Clubs and Societies.

ADDRESS TO THE CATHOLIC ASSOCIATION OF BALTIMORE.

The Catholic Association of Baltimore, under the presidency of the Hon. Richard M. McSherry, gave a public reception to the Delegate at Harris' Academy of Music, on the 15th of April, 1894. On this occasion, the élite of the Monumental City, as if of one accord, gathered to do honor to His Excellency, Mgr. Satolli, and to the Rt. Rev. P. J. Donahue, D. D., who shortly before, had been consecrated Bishop of Wheeling, W. Va. Mr. McSherry with charming felicity, gave greeting to the prelates; Col. Richard Malcolm Johnston, paid a layman's tribute to the Church; Judge Daniel Gans saw in the distinguished gathering an object lesson of which he spoke in glowing terms; the Hon. Charles J. Bonaparte took for his subject, " Higher Education "; after these and before the public exercises were brought to a close by His Eminence, Cardinal Gibbons, Archbishop Satolli delivered the following address:—

Your Eminence, Right Rev. Bishop, Reverend Fathers, Ladies and Gentlemen :—

Four years ago I came to this country for the first time, to be present at the first centenary

203

of the Catholic Hierarchy, celebrated here in Baltimore.

At that time I own that I was surprised at the rapid progress made, not only in the ranks of the hierarchy, but likewise in the extension of Catholicism, outspread as it is, from the Atlantic to the Pacific, from Canada to Mexico.

Four years later, I come again to this country in the official capacity of Apostolic Delegate.

This time I am pleased to say that my surprise is raised to astonishment and admiration, at beholding the conquest made by the Church— a conquest won, not by fire and force, but by truth and morality. These are the two elements that mingle in congenial harmony with the true American spirit.

In saying this, I am giving in one sentence the whole philosophy of history, whence future writers may evolve the true source of America's progress and prosperity.

And may not its past be taken as a happy augury of its future?

During the twenty centuries of its existence, the Church has in no place and at no time found a field so well fitted for the cultivation of the

Christian truth and morality, as right here in America.

This is chiefly due to the wise framing of an equitable Constitution, which guarantees the growth of Christian principles among men.

In the development of the Constitution of the United States, is both the sign and the assurance of the material progress and intellectual advancement of this country.

Man is by his very nature a social being. To prove this the most cogent reason is his inborn yearning, his natural craving, not so much for material progress, as for the moral development of mind and heart. The Catholic Church meets this natural yearning and fosters the social spirit, for she is the mighty promoter of all that aids the culture of art and discipline.

The Catholic Church is endowed with universality and perennial activity, because the life of Jesus Christ has been infused into her, and He has given her the command to spread this life through all generations. He would have her meet all the wants required for human perfectibility.

She obeys this injunction through the preaching of the gospel, and through the agency which faith exercises upon reason and upon the inclinations and desires of the human heart.

Since the inception of the Christian religion the Catholic faith is, and ever has been, necessary for the advancement of civilization. Civilization cannot flourish without its influence. It must root itself in Catholic faith, and be vitalized by it.

As the guest to-night of the Catholic Association of Baltimore, I am glad to speak eulogistic words in behalf of the City of Baltimore, where the Catholic faith flourishes, and with it civilization. When recalling to mind the history of Baltimore, I find it possessed of one excellence that other cities may not claim, and that is, that its origin is Catholic. Hence, Baltimore may aptly be called the Rome of America! And your association shares in this particular honor. Associations differ one from another, but they are readily distinguished by the wants of men—their intelligence, their words and their actions, under the dominion of free will. And as we distinguish science, art and letters by their different objects and aims, so do we divide associations into the three classes that are promotive of the study of science, art and literature.

The excellence and splendor of this association are apparent, for its aim is to cultivate literature and to promote the study of science and art. I praise your association for its cultivation of letters, for literature is the means of keeping alive the social spirit, and is the great medium of spreading Christian truth and morality. But in encouraging the study of literature, I would ask you not to neglect the ancient classic literatures, for in these will you find the models that will guide you along the path of perfection in striving for higher education.

The sciences are either speculative or practical. Metaphysics is the highest speculative science, and I praise your association for its special study of this handmaid of the sciences which gives the standard and criterion to all others. By it universal sciences are made applicable to the most special object that can be offered to the human mind for observation; by it we reach from the material up to the spiritual world. At no period of time has the knowledge of metaphysics been so necessary as it is now. To escape from the extremes of pure idealism or base materialism, to follow in the true course

which knows how happily to combine the rational
and the experimental, is the philosophy, the
Aristotelian philosophy, in its truest sense, which
this age most needs.

The study of the practical sciences of sociology
and political economy is no less necessary if we
are to avoid the degrading position of those
theorists who place the solution of the present-
day social problems in the satisfaction of the
merely useful and material wants of man, to wit,
in riches and physical comforts. Social science
and economics must receive their guidance
from moral philosophy or Christian ethics, for
both the subject and object of these sciences
are man and his actions, and it is utterly
impossible to prescind from morality that which
governs human life in all its ramifications
and relations.

Gladly do I appear here to-night. I would
encourage by my presence, the members of this
Association. You gentlemen, bound together in
harmonious emulation, labor for higher education
and culture. May your efforts towards so great
a good, meet with entire success. I thank your
distinguished president for his gracious greeting

and loyal words; I thank the gifted gentlemen who have spoken so eloquently, and the members of the Association, for the pleasure of being here this evening. May this Association prosper; may it become in Baltimore's diadem, a gem that shall shed its lustre, ever increasing as days roll on their course.

TO THE CATHOLIC CLUB OF PHILADELPHIA.

The eighteenth anniversary of the Catholic Club of Philadelphia deserves to be ranked among the notable Catholic gatherings of the year. It was held on Thursday evening, February 14th, 1895.

His Excellency, Mgr. Satolli, was the guest of honor. Among those present, were His Grace, Archbishop Ryan, the Rt. Rev. Bishop Keane of the Catholic University, the Rt. Rev. Bishop McFaul of Trenton, the Rt. Rev. Bishop Gordon of Jamaica, W. I., Rt. Rev. Mgr. Sbaretti of the Apostolic Delegation, Rev. Dr. F. Z. Rooker, Secretary, and very many others.

Palms in the corners of the room, and bouquets on the tables, added to the festal effect; but the most striking feature of the adornments was a group of pictures, those of the Holy Father, Mgr. Satolli and Archbishop Ryan, hung in the recess on the north wall behind the table reserved for the president of the Club and the guests of honor.

Around them was a profuse draping displaying the American and Papal colors.

His Excellency was toasted by S. E. Megargee, Esq., the President of the Club.

210

In his response, which is unfortunately rather brief, Mgr. Satolli called attention, especially, to one of the beneficial effects of Catholic influence on Society, that of maintaining equilibrium. "The excess of social authority leads to oppression, and the excess of liberty leads to license and the disorganization of the social fabric. The equilibrium of the two constitutes and maintains the life of all Society."

To the great pleasure of being present this evening at the banquet by which you celebrate the eighteenth anniversary of the foundation of this illustrious club, there is united a profound sense of the honor you have paid me. I feel, therefore, constrained by gratitude to express my sincere good wishes and my hope that the prosperity and success of these eighteen years of your club's existence will be followed by a long life, even to centuries, still more fruitful of moral and social benefits, and ever more glorious for this club, which so fittingly ornaments this great city.

The arms of the Catholic Club of Philadelphia appropriately express its character and its aim. In them I see the symbol of heavenly light and the sign of man's redemption by the Man-God; and I read that motto, which is a great principle of social life, " Per Fidem Libertas." This is a solemn declaration against the error of those who think that the sacrifice is incompatible with generous sentiments, and that a clear, well-defined religious faith is irreconcilable with liberty. A renowned writer in science and political economy —Martin of Belgium—has demonstrated both by argument and by facts that justice, charity and sacrifice are the foundation-stones of all free and civilized society, and these three elements are peculiarly the basis of all Christian society; and if a Catholic Club ought to be a concentration of Christian social life, the Catholic Club of Philadelphia surely corresponds to this Christian ideal.

Every historical epoch has its special conflict, and from the sixteenth century down to our own time the conflict has been between liberty and authority. It is the office of religious and social truth to establish harmony between these two terms. The excess of social authority leads to oppression, and the excess of liberty leads to license and the disorganization of the social fabric. The equilibrium of the two constitutes and maintains the life of all society. Proofs are not needed to show that it has ever been the highest glory of the Catholic Church, I do not say to have invented either social authority or social freedom, but to have maintained the equilibrium and established the harmony of the one with the other. And this harmony is what is symbolized in the arms of the Catholic Club of Philadelphia.

I need not tell you how dear to the heart of the Holy Father is the Church in America. I need not tell you the admiration he has for this great American Republic and all her institutions. His Encyclical, which we have so lately received, tells plainly enough his high regard and tender affection for this country. Among the numerous institutions which meet his approval he commends especially the Catholic Clubs, and it is his fervent wish that they should flourish and prosper in every city. This is his desire, because he recognizes the great importance of such organizations. The Catholic Club is an organ of communication between men of varying ages and conditions of life, and between the spirit of religion and the spirit of sociability. Moreover, it facilitates, unifies and strengthens concerted action for the common good, which should never be lacking in religious, domestic and social life. Our Lord said to His disciples that wherever two or three are gathered together in His name, He desired to be considered as being in their midst. We might, in like manner say of our Holy Father, Leo XIII, that he desires to be considered present in all the gatherings held by Catholic clubs. And, therefore, in Catholic clubs a filial affection for the Pope should be cherished in a special manner. The Catholic Club ought to feel that it has a special mission—to teach respect for the Pope in the fulness of his dignity and authority, to sustain him on every occasion, and to aid his plans with regard to the Church and to society. And not only should the Catholic Club universally exhibit the harmony between being a good Catholic and a good citizen, but it should show how one can submit with docility to the teachings of the Pope, and sustain at the same time with all his strength the liberties of his country.

While, then, it will ever remain a happy memory for me that I have taken part in the celebration of your eighteenth anniversary, I shall also be ever persuaded that the Catholic Club of Philadelphia emulates in a special manner other organizations of the kind in its attachment to the Pope, and in its untiring solicitude to perform all that the Pope desires for the welfare of religion and of society.

FIRST ADDRESS TO THE CARROLL INSTITUTE, WASHINGTON, D. C.

On the 30th of January, 1893, the members of the Carroll Institute, Washington, D. C., gave a reception at their hall in honor of the Apostolic Delegate. This speech, delivered by him before a highly distinguished audience, was translated by the Rt. Rev. Bishop Keane of the Catholic University. The erudite rector began by saying that he would give in English the meaning of what the Monsignor had so eloquently expressed in his beautiful Italian, and said what a pity it was that the sin was committed at the Tower of Babel, so that we may not all understand the same language.

"The Papal delegate," he said, "began by saying that while he appreciates every mark of respect and esteem shown him as the legate of the Holy Father, he was particularly gratified at this reception tendered him by a society representing the Catholic gentlemen of this Capital City and bearing the name of one so distinguished in the history of the Church in America. This is an occasion, the memory of which will ever be dear to his heart, and will be a precious memory to

216

the members and to their children, who will be
the future members, and the coming generation,
for it is an occasion linked with so many great
events. It is a significant fact that the opening
of a new chapter in the history of the Institute
should take place in the beginning of a year
marked by so many great events, the sending of
a Papal delegate to this country, the celebration of
the quadro-centenary of the discovery of America
by Christopher Columbus, and the golden jubilee
of Leo XIII.

"It is not strange that the Papal delegate
should give his greeting in Italian, for that was
the language which first sounded over the billows
of the Atlantic and echoed on the shores of
America, when the Italian Columbus bore across
the sea the knowledge of Christ to the shores of
this unknown continent. And it is beautiful to
trace the economy of Divine Providence in the
history of America. The Christian religion,
which was founded by our Divine Saviour at
Jerusalem, was, by Divine Providence, destined
to become centered at Rome. Rome, the greatest
city of the world, was going to destruction on
account of the wickedness of its people, and it

was to become the capital of the Christian world and send forth streams of light to all the nations of the world. Fittingly then, Rome sent Christianity to America just as she received it from Jerusalem, so that the world is encircled by the great chain connecting Jerusalem, Rome, and Washington.

"A study of the history of America, the constitutional organization of our Government, and the sentiments of its founders, as expressed in the writings of Washington and our other great men, only confirm the impression that the life and essence of our institutions are in perfect harmony with the sentiments of our Holy Father Leo XIII on the subject of human liberty.

"In the great event we are so soon to celebrate, three names will be linked together and cherished with love and veneration—the names of Columbus, Washington and Leo XIII. The Papal delegate utters the prediction that as the years unfold and America continues on her great mission, the more closely men analyze the origin and development of her free institutions, the more clearly they will perceive that we are indebted to the teachings and inspirations of the Church of Christ, for all of them."

In conclusion he spoke to this effect : " May your republic, built deep in its foundations of solid rock, raise its pinnacles to the clouds, and like the Church, outlast the ages, and may they side by side, in perpetual good faith and love, teach all mankind true liberty, true brotherhood, and peace everlasting."

PART X.

On the Training of Youth.

ADDRESS TO THE HOLY NAME SOCIETY— PASSIONIST MONASTERY, BALTIMORE.

Mgr. Satolli was invited to bless the new banner of the Holy Name Society at St. Joseph's Passionist Monastery, Frederick Road, Baltimore, Md., the 29th of April, 1893, during the Octave of the feast of St. Paul of the Cross.

On this occasion, the Delegate delivered the following address, speaking in English :—

Much as I am gratified by the solemn reception you gave me, I am more pleased to be called upon to bless the banner of your society.

It is no small matter, rather, I would say, it is of the highest importance that young men should form associations for the common good of religion and country; and the principle of association finds its expression in the banner, the flag, the standard.

There is frequent mention of standards in the Bible.

The Twelve Tribes, when going out of Egypt,

were marshalled under distinctive banners. That of Juda was a lion.

Moses, in the desert, set up the brazen serpent as a symbol of salvation. A somewhat similar device—a rattlesnake on a yellow ensign—was displayed by American warships in the beginning of the Revolution, with the motto:—"Don't Tread upon Me."

The Romans had many standards. At one time, it was the figure of a wolf, the nurse of Romulus, the founder of Rome.

In the time of Marius, an eagle with expanded wings, holding the thunderbolts of Jove in its talons, was set up.

Succeeding emperors displayed new emblems.

Augustus used a globe to symbolize Rome's empire over the world; and Constantine, to commemorate his vision, adopted the Cross, which has come to be regarded as the distinctive symbol of Christendom.

Scripture lays down a truth vital not only to the moral education of youth, but, also to the progress of society, when it says:—"A young man according to his way; even when he is old, he will not depart from it."

As the young shoots in the garden are easily tended, and later produce good fruit in abundance, so youth has the promises of vigor and prosperity for every society.

The history of all nations shows that their founders and lawgivers gave their first and chiefest care to the bringing up of youth.

So true is this, that if one wished to put in one word the characteristic difference of the various commonwealths of Sparta, Athens and Rome, he needs but know what were the laws and customs of each in the education of the rising generation.

In this very field of work lies the immortal glory of Lycurgus, Solon, Numa Pompilius.

The one would have youth pre eminent in war, the other would have youth pre-eminent in mental culture, the third would have young men lovers of liberty and masters of the world.

The Hebrew race, too, had its characteristic method and features of education pointed out by the Divine Spirit to Moses and other wise leaders, especially Sirach, the writer of the book of Ecclesiasticus, wherein he has given, not only for his own race, but for every race that aims at

15

moral life and true progress, most beautiful and salutary principles on the training of youth.

But far above and beyond those, or any others, who have dealt with this problem, is our Lord Jesus Christ, Who, though Son of God, deigned to become Son of Man, Who from boyhood grew to youth, and from youth to that manhood through which He redeemed mankind and re-made the nations.

Everywhere in Scripture He seems to be say-ing, oftener by implication than expressly:—"Let the little ones, let youth come to Me, for of such is the kingdom of Heaven."

Now, in regard to our youths, there are three rights, which have claims upon them, viz., the right of nature, the right of the nation, and the right of God; that is, for domestic society under the rule of parents, for civil society under the rule of due authority, and for the Church of Christ, under the sway of Divine authority.

This last is of all societies the greatest by ex-tent, dignity and faith.

It is evident, then, that out of this triple fountain must flow the quality that makes good and efficacious the education of youth.

Moreover, since arts and sciences are not to be dissociated from morality, and morality is not to be had without religion, and religion is Christian, and Christianity has its completeness, and its real life, past, present and future, in the Catholic Church; it follows that the constant care, the aim of our united forces should be, that our Catholic young men in their associations should be thoroughly imbued with Catholic truth and morality.

This, then, is the reason and meaning of associations of Catholic young men banded beneath the banner of this or of some other patron.

Already your country knows by experience how useful the Church is to her, and how much the Church may contribute to her future solidity and glory.

The Republic is now fully aware and convinced that her best hopes are centered in that generation, who have received and are receiving Christian training, Christian faith and morality alongside of secular knowledge—for the inevitable fruits of moral and Christian training are justice, charity and peace.

Above all, let us understand that civil liberty cannot endure without the liberty of Christ, the true liberty, by which He has made us free.   For, how can man be said to be free, or remain free, when he is so only in appearance, when he wears only the mask of liberty, when, in reality, he is a slave to his passions, and, like a beast, is led blindly by his sensual appetites.

May God bless and protect you, Catholic young men.   May the patrons of your societies bestow their intercessions in your behalf, that you may be firm in the purposes, cheerful and constant in the duties of your associations.

In conclusion, let me beg you to take with you the assurance that the better grounded you are as Catholics in faith and morals, as becomes Catholics, the more prudent, honest and useful citizens you will make of this great Republic of the United States.

AT THE CLOSE OF A MISSION

AT THE CHURCH OF ST. MARY MAGDALEN DE PAZZI,
PHILADELPHIA.

On Palm Sunday, March 26th, 1893, at the close of a Mission which Mgr. Satolli gave in the Italian Church above named, he gave a special address to the young people of the parish, including the Holy Childhood Society, the Children of Mary, and the Columbus Societies.

Master Ciangolini read an address in Italian, to which Monsignor Satolli replied in his native tongue, after which the Papal Delegate read an address in the English language.

His voice, clearly enunciating every syllable, was heard distinctly throughout the church, and the address was listened to with the greatest interest. Among other things he said:—

The most interesting portion of Christianity is composed of young people—yourselves.

The sight of the earnest young faces I have seen in this church during the past week—for a great part of my audiences has been made up of young people—has gladdened my heart.

I sincerely trust that you will keep fresh in
your memory the many salutary truths which I
have preached to you, and that you will act in
conformity to the Christian spirit recommended
to you by me.

You are in the midst of many and strong
temptations. You have the false liberty to do
evil, but you have also the true liberty to do
good; hence you are inexcusable if you fail in
your duties. Remember always that the duties
of a Christian must be invariably above his
material interests Remember also, when one
neglects his religious duties, God often punishes
it by the loss of our material interests. Misfortunes of one kind or another always follow
the guilty transgression of the law of God and
the neglect of one's religious duties.

It was said of old that the Christians were the
soul of the world. So now we should be able to
say that the Christians are the soul of America.

Much is said in our days of social assimilation with those who dwell in this great country.
Assimilation must be spontaneous, gradual, for
the common good of all parts composing the
social body. It must be neither violent nor

strained. You must distinguish well the civil
from the religious assimilation; because, if in the
civil assimilation we must go to others, in the
religious one we must wait for the others to come
to us. In regard to religious sentiment and
matters of faith, and in regard to truly Catholic
morals and every observance of the Catholic religion, we must hold firm.

True Catholics lead an honest life. It is better
to be well educated than to be simply instructed.
Nay, for us Catholics, education that is not Catholic, in a moral sense, is impossible. This is the
supreme reason for parochial schools, namely, for
those schools of ours which, besides teaching all
that is useful to the domestic and civil interest,
perfect it by means of moral and religious education.

Hence it is, that while Catholics respect the
civil institutions, they have their own rights and
their own schools. They deserve that public
opinion should be favorable to them, and justly
hope for the co-operation of all honest people.
The loyalty of men to the principles laid down
by the American Constitution, and their sense of
justice, we have reason to hope, will not allow

them to consider such schools as anti-American, as they are in full accord with all that a free and civil State can demand.

The future of America is bright, and Church and State meet in a friendly way. The Constitution of the United States does not contain any law concerning religious matters, but wants all citizens to be law-abiding and God-fearing, and wants one and the same freedom for all, and no one of the religious professions, outside of the Catholic, is better suited to American liberty than it is. Beware especially of pernicious readings as of deadly poison.

Finally, in token of my best wishes, and of the pleasure which it has afforded me to be among you, with all my heart, and in the name of our Holy Father, Leo XIII, I give you all, and to your families also, my special Apostolic blessing.

AT THE PASSIONIST MONASTERY, WEST HOBOKEN, N. J.

On May 14th, 1894, His Excellency blessed a statue of Saint Aloysius at the Passionist Monastery, West Hoboken, N. J. He spoke to a large gathering of the parish children and their parents, as follows:

My dear children, one of the earliest and sweetest memories of my own childhood, is connected with such a ceremony as this in which we are now engaged. I remember, as if it been but yesterday, that I was chosen from among my boy companions to be the orator, to tell the praises of Saint Aloysius on a feast gotten up in his honor.

It is a pleasure to me to take part in a ceremony of the same kind in this great republic, in this parish, so zealously governed by the Passionist Fathers. Beneath this dome, which reminds me of the classic church of fair Italy, in the presence of this company of children whose society is dedicated to the memory of Saint

Aloysius, and bears his name, I seem to be carried far back into other years, and to live over again, days long past.

Many indeed, have been the statues erected and unveiled with pomp and music during this memorable year, in this country; countless and splendid the processions in honor of the immortal discoverer of America. What is the purpose and the meaning of this deep and widespread enthusiasm in honor of Columbus?

Is it only to express admiration and gratitude for his wonderful achievement which made possible the American Republic? Is it only that this republic, with its progressive civilization, with its grand church to which the gaze of the whole world is directed, and on which universal expectations for future ages depend, is it, I ask you, that this republic may show to other nations how to render homage to the good, the true, the brave?

Certainly, this has been one motive, but not the only one. There has been a higher, nobler purpose. That nobler purpose is to put before the youth of this land a model of exalted ambition. enlightened and directed by faith, of cour-

ageous perseverance in a grand course, which
overcame all obstacles, a model of generosity
reaching unto the sacrifice of wealth, comfort,
even life itself, for disgrace and poverty were the
only rewards which the finding of a world brought
to him in his old age.

Surely, the lessons conveyed by Columbus' life
are the rational meaning and purpose of this
universal civic cult that mark our history in this
year of our Lord 1892.

I am about to bless a statue of Saint Aloysius,
to be set up in your noble church, and, as I now
speak to you, I would recall to your minds that
your great poet Shakespeare has said, that there
are sermons in stones.

This statue of the patron saint of youth, will
stand here to preach you a constant sermon.

The first duty of man is to love God, and this
love shows itself in two ways, namely. respect for
God's Holy Name; respect and charity for our
fellow-men, made in the image of God.

St. Aloysius never pronounced the name of the
Almighty without the deepest reverence, nor
could he bear to hear it profaned by others.

St. Aloysius carried his charity for his neighbors to that point, which St. Paul has marked—he would be anathema for his brethren.

There lies on children as such, no duty greater than reverence for their parents, and obedience to their just demands.

St. Aloysius saw in his parents the representatives of God, and never failed in his respect for them. The loveliest virtue of youth is chastity of mind and body, and modesty of demeanor. St. Aloysius was an angel among men; he walked unsinged amid the fires of sensuality, and spread about him the sweet odor of heavenly purity.

The main occupation of early years is to gain knowledge and to pursue courageously the prize of education. St. Aloysius spent his short life in the study of things temporal and eternal, and, because of this he will forever be the model of the Catholic student. To rise above the attractions of wealth, to be superior to high social position, to strive for things nobler than these, noble though they be, especially when they come as the rewards of effort, indicate strength of purpose, elevation of ideals, and manliness of the first order.

St. Aloysius ever saw before him an end more glorious than earthly prosperity. For the sake of elevating mankind, of gaining heaven, of living in, and with God, he laid aside his ancestral coronet, renounced his dukedom, spurned wealth, and became the humble novice of that religious order whose aim is expressed by their motto: "All for the greater glory of God."

All this the statue I am about to bless will tell you, and much more that I have not time to specify. Children of St. Aloysius, study the life of your patron and strive to imitate him. Like him be respectful to God and man. Be obedient to your parents, be pure, studious, have the noble ambition of things superior to earth!

If ever it be your good fortune to go to Rome do not fail, after a visit to the tomb of the great Apostles, Peter and Paul, to go to the shrine of St. Aloysius in the Church of St. Ignatius, not far from that grandest of Christian monuments that covers the venerated remains of the founders of Christian Rome.

May he from his bright throne in heaven look down on you, and bless you, and give you that superhuman courage that made him the saint he is.

PART XI.

Letters.

TO THE GERMAN CATHOLIC CENTRAL SOCIETY.

His Excellency, who was unable to be present at the Convention of the German Catholic Central Society, held in New York city, September 17th, 1894, sent the following letter:

WASHINGTON, *September 4th*, 1894.

CONRAD STRASSBURGER.

Dear Sir:—I have received your kind favor informing me of the next meeting of the German Roman Catholic Central Verein, to be held in New York, and inviting me to take part in the same. The spirit of association aiming at the attainment of the religious, social and moral welfare of the people is a spirit belonging preeminently to the Catholic church. This church, after securing peace to the world and forming Catholic nations, showed at once an inexplicable fecundity of engendering the innumerable insti-

16 241

tutions of the monastic life of the most various
kinds according to the different wants of places
and ages. This same church has brought into
life among the Catholic laymen, brotherhoods
and associations for all kinds of professions, arts
and sciences, for benevolent purposes, and for all
the needs of the domestic and civil life.

During this century the enemies of the Catholic church have tried every manner of means to
destroy these institutions, and they have done
nothing but heap up ruins. However, the Catholic church is still alive; she infused the breath of
her life into those ruins according to the new
times. She soon created also new forms of Catholic associations. The enemies of the church
labored for the secularization of Catholicism, and
even of christendom, and the Catholics have
answered by Catholic congresses. And thus those
powers which the enemies wished to separate and
destroy through said congresses, have been united
and strengthened. This story of Germany shall
have golden pages to record the institution and
the advantages of the Catholic congresses, from
which sprang the Catholic center, that body
which was the primary cause of the collapse

more or less complete of the sadly famous kulturkampf.

It was, therefore, to be expected that the German Catholics emigrating to this country, should come with the torch of faith in their hands and the spirit of brotherhood and association in their hearts, and that thus they would be most diligent in founding Catholic associations and celebrating congresses. The character of Catholic congresses requires that they should harmonize with the spirit of the Church and the country; and they prove very useful whenever, being celebrated under the patronage of the ecclesiastical authorities, such resolutions are adopted by them as are required by the interests of the Catholic faith and the conditions of social life. Certainly, the usefulness and necessity of such societies and conventions can easily be proved by the salutary effects already achieved through them. Nay, only malice or ignorance could prevent anybody from recognizing their need and utility, since the Holy Father has recommended them so strongly.

Therefore, please to accept the sincere expression of my high esteem for your present convention and my congratulations for the whole society on the great good already affected by the same, especially through its congresses in protecting the faith and morality and even the material interests of the Catholic Germans in the United States. Please also to accept my best wishes for your next congress, and be sure that, although I cannot take part in it personally, my heart will be among you, by imploring from heaven the choicest blessings upon all of you in my name, and in the name of the Holy Father himself. Yours truly in Christ,

FRANCIS, ARCHBISHOP SATOLLI,
Delegate Apostolic.

ON THE SEVENTEENTH ANNIVERSARY OF THE CORONATION OF LEO XIII.

To the Editor of The New York World:

The Pontificate of Pope Leo must now be numbered among the longest in the history of the Church and has been marked each year by some luminous act of profound wisdom and untiring solicitude for the good, not only of Catholicity, but of mankind at large.

No one in modern times has understood better than Pope Leo the needs of society in all branches of knowledge and fields of action.

It would seem as if, from the time when he succeeded Pope Pius, he had formed a grand plan, in which he took cognizance of all the needs of humanity and determined on the provisions he would make for those needs during the whole course of his Pontificate.

We can best distinguish this design of the Pope, in three particular directions.

Firstly, in the Holy Father's ardent zeal for the development of studies.

Secondly, in the continued interest which he has shown in social science.

And thirdly, in his untiring efforts to bring peace into the Christian countries by the spread of civilization, the teaching of religion and the promotion of concord between Church and State.

With regard to studies, Pope Leo has already reared a monument of imperishable fame by the successive acts of his Pontificate.

Early in his reign he turned his attention to the encouragement of the study of classical litera-ture; of philosophy and the natural sciences; of theology and the various branches of sacred sciences, such as Biblical knowledge and ecclesi-astical history; and of judicial sciences, especially of Roman law and comparative civil law.

To accomplish his aim he founded new chairs and new institutions in Rome for these various departments of literary and encyclopaedic know-ledge, and called to his assistance some of the most eminent and learned professors.

With regard to sociology, it is another of the Holy Father's glories that at this latter end of the

nineteenth century his encyclicals are regarded
as so many admirable parts of a grand doctrinal
system, comprehensive and universal, embracing
all the social sciences, beginning with the fundamental theorems of natural law and going on to
the consideration of the political constitution of
States and of every economic question.

The whole world knows how well the Pope's
encyclicals have carried out his plan, and how,
for this reason, they have their own peculiar
character by which they are distinguished from
the Pontifical utterances of other Popes, even
those of his immediate predecessor, Pius the
Ninth.

Turning again to his policy of pacification, the
ecclesiastical history of his Pontificate, the civil
history of Europe, the universal history of the
human race, will in the future have to give up
pages of the highest praise to Leo XIII.

Germany, Belgium, France and Spain profess
their boundless gratitude for the peace-giving
interventions of Leo XIII in many grave and
critical emergencies, and for acts which have been
of the greatest moment to those nations.

Asia, too, and Africa, will be found joining in

the chorus, and lauding Leo, who has so often
and so resolutely labored to reawaken those old
and fossilized portions of the earth to a new life
of Christian civilization.

Nor will America, throughout its length and
breadth, withhold its tribute of loyal and generous veneration, esteem and gratitude to Pope
Leo for those acts of his Pontificate which have
at various times been promulgated, and by which
he has shown his confidence and hope in the
grand future of this mighty nation.

During the seventeen years of his pontifical
rule nothing has been more. remarkable or plain
than the incessant growth of his benignant moral
influence.

To-day the Holy Father's words are listened
to with deference by every court, by every Government, by every people.

On every question touching universal human
interests his counsel is sought eagerly, and welcomed gratefully.

Despite, then, all the adverse trend of mundane
circumstances, despite the loss of the external
symbols of its high authority, the Papacy has
gained in power and splendor since the accession

of the present glorious Pontiff. As Macaulay says in one of his most noble essays:

"The Papacy remains, not in decay, not a mere antique, but full of life and youthful vigor."

FRANCIS, ARCHBISHOP SATOLLI,
Delegate Apostolic.

WASHINGTON, *March* 2, 1895.